15 MINUTE DEVOTIONS for COUPLES

Bob & Emilie Barnes

HARVEST HOUSE PUBLISHERS

EUGENE, OREGON

Cover by Dugan Design Group, Bloomington, Minnesota

15 MINUTE DEVOTIONS FOR COUPLES

Copyright © 1995 by Harvest House Publishers
Eugene, Oregon 97402
www.harvesthousepublishers.com

Library of Congress Cataloging-in-Publication Data

Barnes, Bob, 1933–
    15 minute devotions for couples / Bob and Emilie Barnes
        p. cm.
    ISBN 978-0-7369-1203-7 (pbk.)
    ISBN 978-0-7369-3245-5 (eBook)

    1. Married people—Prayer–books and devotions—English.
    I. Barnes, Emilie. II. Title.
    BV4596.M3B37   1995
    242'.644—dc20   95-44190
                                                 CIP

Printed in the United States of America

16   17   18   19   20   21   / BP /   18   17   16   15   14   13

This book is dedicated to all the couples who commit their 15-minute blocks of time each day to read these thoughts. Over the years we have come to realize that our bonding and mutual love for each other have grown when we do things together. You will find that this daily block of time will give you a better feeling of direction and joint commitment to your life purposes.

If time permits, do the "Taking Action" section together. Discuss the questions and delve into your mate's innermost thoughts about these activities. This block of time will help satisfy your common concern, "We never talk about anything!" These activities will help you bridge the communication gap if you have one. Through these devotions you will begin to see God doing a marvelous work in your lives. Each of your hearts will be opened to the other, and you will become more transparent in your lives.

You will begin talking about things you never thought possible. These discussions will have heavenly purpose and will open the door of your heart to let the Holy Spirit talk to both of you in new ways.

Even if you aren't a couple, but a single person, a single parent, or a single grandparent, you will find great challenges and insights in these pages.

May the Lord bless you as you read this book!

15 Minute Devotions for Couples

As we enter the last part of the '90s, God is at work among couples in America in a mighty way. More and more couples are hearing and responding to His call. Many are naming Jesus as their Lord and Savior for the first time, and others are rededicating themselves to the Lord. If these commitments are to make a significant impact on our families, our nation, and our world, they need to be nourished daily, and that, we pray, is where this book comes in.

One way we sustain our commitment to the Lord is to read His Word daily. The material in this devotional is designed to challenge and encourage couples in their spiritual journey by getting them into God's Word. In each of the following 15-minute entries you'll read a passage in Scripture and a short devotion based on that selection, pray about what you've read, and then be challenged to act on what you've learned.

Don't worry about reading the book from front to back. Skip around if you like. In the upper right-hand corner on the first page of each entry you'll find three boxes. Put a checkmark in one of the boxes each time you read it. In this way you can keep track of those devotions which you have read previously. But keep in mind that if you consistently spend 15 minutes a day for several weeks, you'll be on the way toward a lifelong habit of spending a few moments alone with God every day.

May the Lord richly bless you as you listen for and respond to His call, living on a higher plain than those around you. One of the cements that holds couples together is a joint commitment to common values and activities. Let this book be a part of that shared interest!

—Bob and Emilie Barnes

We are in too big a hurry, and we run by far more than we catch up with. The Bible tells us to "be still, and know that I am God" (Psalm 46:10 KJV). Beauty doesn't shout. Loveliness is quiet. Our finest moods are not clamorous. The familiar appeals of the Divine are always in calm tones—a still, small voice.

—*Charles L. Allen*

The Stability of Your Life

Scripture Reading: Isaiah 33:1-12

Key Verse: Isaiah 33:6

> *He will be the sure foundation for your times, a rich store of salvation and wisdom and knowledge; the fear of the Lord is the key to this treasure.*

———— ✍ ————

This week we received a letter from a dear friend whom we financially support in her ministry. She has expressed over the months that God has been guiding her in new ways but the light to the path isn't clear yet. She expresses changes on the horizons and isn't sure of what lies ahead, but her letter is a continuation of her search for new direction. She shares in her letter:

> At this point in my life I am facing changes in many respects, and if I did not know the Lord and if I did not know that He establishes and directs my steps, I could be shaken by some of what I see happening around me (Psalm 37:23; Proverbs 16:9).

As I was thanking Him just a few days ago for the fact that I know He is the same yesterday, today, and forever (Hebrews 13:8) and that although circumstances and relationships may change, He never changes nor forsakes me (Hebrews 13:5). He brought a verse to my mind that I have known over the years. Through this verse He has also brought comfort to me for these changing times I am in. The verse is Isaiah 33:6: "He shall be the stability of your times" (NASB).

Isn't it a comfort to know truths that confirm His faithfulness to us, and then in addition to realize that He is our stability!

The word *stability* means the strength to stand or endure; firmness; the property of a body that causes it, when disturbed from a condition of equilibrium, to develop forces that restore the original condition.

What a promise! When we may feel shaken, He is firm and stands and endures for us! He is that which will always restore us to a condition of equilibrium, no matter what!

If you are not now in a situation in which changing circumstances are a factor, then you may not appreciate fully what this promise has meant to me in these last days, but you know a time will come when changes will be a factor, and, as I said earlier, then you will want to embrace this truth. It will hold you with hope and confidence in a state of changes!

Thank you again for your faithfulness!

Here is one person who can recall and claim God's mighty Scriptures to see us through difficult times. Even though our stability is shaken in the present, He promises that He will always be the same—never wavering.

Changes become a factor in all of our lives. If not today, then surely tomorrow or the next day. Isn't it wonderful to know that when changes come we can go to God's Word to find the strength to see us through another situation! Let's not wait for the storm to seek verses that comfort and direct, but let's be prepared when these days appear on the horizon (and they surely will) and have these fantastic truths in our memory bank.

Prayer

Father God, we do not know when changes will appear, but we know they will. Prepare in our hearts those Scriptures that will give us everlasting promises. Make us aware as we read these Scriptures to pick out those that will strengthen our faith in You. We don't want to wait before we seek. We want to have hidden in our hearts those verses which give us assurance that You will be there in time of need. Thank You, God, for taking care of all the needs of the past, the present, and most assuredly the future. Amen.

Taking Action

- Memorize Isaiah 33:6.

- List in your journal five events in your life in which God has provided.

- Trust that He can be trusted for your future situations.

- Do you see any future changes for you and your family? What are they? What verses will help you through these changes?

Reading On

Psalm 37:23	Proverbs 16:9
Hebrews 13:8	Psalm 42:11

What Is Success?

Scripture Reading: Obadiah 1:2-7
Key Verse: Obadiah 1:3

> *The pride of your heart has deceived you, you who live in the clefts of the rocks and make your home on the heights, you who say to yourself, "Who can bring me down on the ground?"*

Last summer our family rented a modest cabin at Lake Arrowhead in the San Bernardino mountains about one hour from our home. It was going to be a quiet getaway to read, rest, and relax. We don't get to do these three R's enough.

During the course of the three days up there, my attention was drawn to a dusty old framed verse that skipped my attention until day two. It hung in one of the bathrooms, and as I took time to read it my eyes came across this collection of thoughts on success:

> Great people are just ordinary people with an extra-ordinary amount of determination.... There is no gain without pain. When you fail to plan, you plan to fail.... Change your

thoughts and you can change your world. There are infinite possibilities in little beginnings if God is in them. Build a dream and the dream will build you. Inch by inch, anything is a cinch. I am God's project and God never fails. Don't let impossibilities intimidate you, do let possibilities motivate you. Make your decisions on "God's ability," not your ability. What you are is God's gift to you; what you make of yourself is your gift to God. It's possible to face the music with God's song in your heart. God's delays are not God's denials. I'd rather attempt to do something great and fail than attempt to do nothing and succeed.... Look at what you have left, not at what you have lost. Find a hurt and heal it. You are God's project and God never fails.

As I finished reading these collections of clever thoughts I began to think upon this concept of success. Today our media tries to bombard us with all the materialism of the universe to make us compare our adventure with all that the world has to offer. My first thoughts were that if material success brought happiness then all the wealthy people of the world would be very happy and all the poor people would be very sad, but that's really the opposite of what I've observed in life.

Then I said to myself, "Then what is success?" A quote from the past flashed through my brain: "Success is progressive realization of worthwhile goals!" Yes, that's the whole idea of success.

That must mean my wife and I have to sit down and think through some worthwhile goals and we must attain

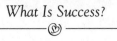
them over a period of time. They aren't instantly attainable; they are progressively realized—postponed gratifications, if you will.

Two common barriers that prevent most people from reaching their goals is 1) we have made a habit of past failures and mistakes, and 2) we fear failure. Because of these two negatives, many of us never reach our potential.

As you and your spouse think through today's thoughts you may want to do some homework on your definition of success.

Prayer

> *Father God, may You put a protective hedge around our home so we won't be dragged down by the fears of the past. As Christians we can be confident that our past has been forgiven. Those mistakes need not hold us back. Since You are sovereign, You know the beginning from the end—You are in complete control of our lives. We can believe your promise found in Romans 8:28.*
>
> *Permit our energies to focus on the present and the future and not to be hung up over the failures of the past.*
>
> *Free us to think positively on worthwhile goals. Amen.*

Taking Action

- You and your spouse write a short statement regarding your purpose for life.

- You and your spouse sit down and write out two goals for each of the following areas of your life:

☐ Spiritual
☐ Professional
☐ Financial
☐ Family
☐ Home
☐ Leisure
☐ Health

- After each goal write down the quantity of each and a date when you want it to be accomplished (e.g., we want to save 500 dollars by the first of December). These two qualities of a goal are very important because with them you can measure how you did by the first of December.

- List two or three activities that you will do to accomplish these goals.

- Check back each month to see how you are doing in these areas.

Reading On

Romans 8:28
Romans 10:1-13
Isaiah 55:1-7

What to Count

Don't count how many years
    you've spent,
Just count the good
    you've done;
The times you've lent
    a helping hand,
The friends that you have won.
Count your deeds of kindness,
The smiles, not the tears;
Count all the pleasures
    that you've had,
But never count the years.

Just Keep On Pedaling

Scripture Reading: Proverbs 3:1-8

Key Verses: Proverbs 3:5-6

> *Trust in the Lord with all your heart and lean not on your own understanding; in all your ways acknowledge him, and he will make your paths straight.*

At first I saw God as my observer, my judge, keeping the things I did wrong, so as to know whether I merited heaven or hell when I die. He was out there sort of like the President. I knew He was out there, but I didn't really know Him.

But later on when I recognized God, it seemed as though life was rather like a bike ride, but it was a tandem bike, and I noticed that God was in the back helping me pedal.

I don't know just when it was that He suggested we change places, but life has not been the same since. Life without my God, that is. God makes life exciting!

When I had control, I knew the way. It was rather boring, but predictable. It was the shortest distance between two points. But when He took the lead, He knew delightful long cuts, up mountains, through rocky places, and at breakneck speeds! It was all I could do to hang on! Even though it looked like madness, He said, "Pedal!"

I worried and was anxious and asked, "Where are you taking me?" He laughed and didn't answer. I started to learn to trust. I forgot my boring life and entered into the adventure. And when I'd say "I'm scared," He'd lean back and touch my hand.

He took me to people with gifts that I needed—the gifts of healing, acceptance, and joy. They gave me their gifts to take on my journey—our journey, God's and mine. And we were off again. He said, "Give the gifts away. They're extra baggage, too much weight." So I did, to the people we met, and I found that in giving I received, and still our burden was light.

I did not trust Him in control of my life at first. I thought He'd wreck it. But He knows bike secrets. He knows how to make it bend to take sharp corners, jump to clear high rocks, fly to shorten scary passages.

And I am learning to shut up and pedal in the strangest places, and I'm beginning to enjoy the view and the cool breeze on my face with my delightful constant companion, my God.

And when I'm sure I just can't do any more, He smiles and says, "Pedal."[1]

When some people say, "Oh, life is so boring I don't even want to get up in the morning," we can't comprehend that kind of travel. We find life so exciting that our feet bound out of bed each day anticipating what God has in store for us.

Each day is a real adventure. Many days God just says, "Come along and trust me." It would be nice to know every detail, what lies beyond each ridge and what's around each of the corners of life, but God very patiently says, "Just trust me. You do the pedaling and I'll do the leading." Our reply is often, "Are you sure You know the way? What if You make a mistake with my life? But, God, I've never been this way before. What if . . . ." The dialogue can go on for hours, days, and months, but eventually we arrive to the point where we say, "God, You lead and I'll keep on pedaling."

As our key verse says today, we are to trust in the Lord with all our heart and not on our own understanding. That's so hard to do if we're not used to turning over our lives to Someone who is bigger than us. Just relax and let God be all that He says He is—TRUSTWORTHY.

Prayer

Father God, you know how hard it is for us to let go and let God. We human beings are so used to being in control. We have a very difficult time in trusting anyone else; especially someone we can't even see and touch. Please stay close to us when we doubt. It's not that we don't want to trust, it's just that this is so new to us. Please be patient with our little steps, for one day we will be able to run and not stumble, but today we feel like a young child who is just beginning to crawl. Amen.

Taking Action

- List in your journal four things that have been bothering you and your spouse and that you want to give to God.

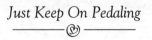
- Read the additional verses that are given in the next section. See how you can apply them to your four situations.

- Share with your mate what these four situations are— be transparent enough to risk being small in the sight of your spouse.

Reading On

> Psalm 46:1,2
> 1 Peter 5:7
> Matthew 6:31,32
> Psalm 40:4

My Gift of Love

My loving you can never be an abdication of my own self. I could possibly give my life for you out of love, but I could never deny my identity as a person. I will try to be what you need me to be, to do what you need done, to say whatever you need to hear. At the same time I am committed to an honest and open relationship. As a part of my gift of love, I will always offer my thoughts, preferences, and all my feelings, even when I think they may be unpleasant or even hurtful to your feelings.

—John Powell

Have You Read the Book

Scripture Reading: 2 Timothy 3:10-17
Key Verse: 2 Timothy 3:16

> *All Scripture is God-breathed and is useful for teaching, rebuking, correcting and training in righteousness.*

———————— ⌾ ————————

In a recent letter from Wycliffe Bible Translators, we received from Hyatt Moore, Director, a communique stating:

> In 1835 Harvard scholar Richard Henry Dana took time off from his studies and went to sea for his health. It almost broke him. From his experiences he wrote *Two Years Before the Mast*, the first account of life at sea written from the perspective of a common seaman.
>
> It was a very hard life, often dangerous, usually uncomfortable, the food unchanging, and human contact sparse. Working the West Coast collecting hides (for shoes in the East), Dana wrote, "Here we were, in a little vessel, with a small crew, on a half-civilized coast, at the ends of the earth. . . ." He was in Santa Barbara, California.
>
> To make matters worse, the captain was tyrannical. Punishing a small infraction with brutal whipping

was not beyond him. On ship there was no other law, no redress, no way out. It was these kinds of experiences that caused Dana to vow, were he ever to get back to America (California was still part of Mexico), that he would dedicate himself to lighten the sufferings of this poor class of people, one of which he had become.

In fact that is what happened. Dana later took up maritime law and saw through some significant changes.

Since then Dana has been pretty much forgotten. There's a town by his name along the California coast, with his statue, a replica of his ship, and curiosities for tourists. But if people haven't read his book they don't know his story—and most haven't.

In a way there's a parallel between what Dana did for seamen and what the Lord did for us all. He came and identified with the poor, working, suffering, and dedicating himself to the solution of our pains. In the years since then statues have been erected and memorabilia have been sold, but a great many people still don't know much about our Lord. Most haven't read His book.[2]

As a couple it is very important that we establish a time where we can individually or collectively get into God's Word and see what He has for us in it.

Sometimes we have insurance, credit cards, and membership policies that grant us privileges we know nothing about, because we haven't taken the time to read all the benefits we have through being a member in good standing of a certain organization. That's the way it is with the Bible.

We miss out on some great blessings because we haven't taken the time to read the Book.

Here are a few blessings to consider:

- God so loved the world that he gave his one and only Son, that whoever believes in him shall not perish but have eternal life (John 3:16).

- To all who received him, to those who believed in his name, he gave the right to become children of God (John 1:12).

- He who is kind to the poor lends to the Lord, and he will reward him for what he has done (Proverbs 19:17).

- He gives strength to the weary and increases the power of the weak (Isaiah 40:29).

- The fruit of the Spirit is love, joy, peace, patience, kindness, goodness, faithfulness, gentleness and self-control (Galatians 5:22).

- The fear of the Lord adds length to life, but the years of the wicked are cut short (Proverbs 10:27).

Don't let another day go by in your Christian walk without taking the time to discover at least one new promise for the day. A good beginning is reading the books of Psalms and Proverbs. Each verse you will want to have engraved on your brain, for each is so inspirational. Many of them appear on plaques or greeting cards. You may say, "I've read that before, but I didn't realize it came from the Bible."

Prayer

Father God, thank You for letting us read this thought for today. We have needed a little prodding to get our engines started. We earnestly want to get into Your Word each day. May our desires become a priority for each day. As a couple may we hold each other accountable to read Your Book each day, and when possible we might share together the highlights of our study. We look forward to what You will teach us each day. Amen.

Taking Action

- Confirm with your spouse that you want to be held accountable to read God's Word daily.

- Share with each other daily (you choose the most convenient time and place) what God has been revealing to you through His Word.

- Enter into your journal each day a few truths that you are learning.

- Try to memorize the key verse in your passage. Write the verse on a 3x5 card and take it with you everywhere so you can review between those few spare moments we all have.

Reading On

Romans 1:16
Deuteronomy 11:18
Revelation 1:3
Joshua 1:8

Not Yet

Scripture Reading: James 1:2-12

Key Verses: James 1:2-4

> *Consider it pure joy, my brothers, whenever you face trials of many kinds, because you know that the testing of your faith develops perseverance. Perseverance must finish its work so that you may be mature and complete, not lacking anything.*

There was a couple who used to go to England to shop in the beautiful stores. This was their twenty-fifth wedding anniversary. They both liked antiques and pottery and especially teacups. One day in this beautiful shop they saw a beautiful teacup. They said, "May we see that? We've never seen one quite so beautiful." As the lady handed it to them, suddenly the teacup spoke.

"You don't understand," it said. "I haven't always been a teacup. There was a time when I was red and I was clay. My master took me and rolled me and patted me over and over and I yelled out, 'Let me alone,' but he only smiled, 'Not yet.'

"Then I was placed on a spinning wheel," the teacup said, "and suddenly I was spun around and around and around. 'Stop it! I'm getting dizzy!' I screamed. But the master only nodded and said, 'Not yet.'

"Then he put me in the oven. I never felt such heat. I wondered why he wanted to burn me, and I yelled, and I knocked at the door. I could see him through the opening and I could read his lips as he shook his head, 'Not yet.'

"Finally the door opened, he put me on the shelf, and I began to cool. 'There, that's better,' I said. And he brushed and painted me all over. The fumes were horrible. I thought I would gag. 'Stop it, stop it!' I cried. He only nodded, 'Not yet.'

"Then suddenly he put me back into the oven, not like the first one. This was twice as hot and I knew I would suffocate. I begged. I pleaded. I screamed. I cried. All the time I could see him through the opening nodding his head, saying, 'Not yet.'

"Then I knew there wasn't any hope. I would never make it. I was ready to give up. But the door opened and he took me out and placed me on the shelf. One hour later he handed me a mirror and said, 'Look at yourself.' And I did. I said, 'That's not me; that couldn't be me. It's beautiful. I'm beautiful.'

"'I want you to remember, then,' he said, 'I know it hurt to be rolled and patted, but if I just left you, you'd have dried up. I know it made you dizzy to spin around on the wheel, but if I had stopped, you would have crumbled. I know it hurt and it was hot and disagreeable in the oven, but if I hadn't put you there, you would have cracked. I know the fumes were bad when I brushed and painted you all over, but if I hadn't done that, you never would have hardened. You would not have had any color in your life, and if I hadn't put you back in that second oven, you wouldn't survive for very long because the hardness would not have held. Now you are a finished product. You are what I had in mind when I first began with you.'"[3]

As a couple we will face many adversities in life. Trials that will attempt to split us apart—separate us from our children, our in-laws, our churches, and even our businesses. That's life! Some of us are in the oven screaming, hollering, kicking on the door, and yelling, "Let me out of here! I can't take it any longer!" Some of us are in the glaze stage and are getting our final paint job. The fumes and stench are bothering us and making our heads go in circles. A few of us are going round and round on the spinning wheel. We are disoriented and just want off. It's got to stop someday, so we figure it might as well be today.

Everything's a mess, and God keeps saying, "Not yet, not yet."

How much do you trust God with your life? Do you have a big box or a little box for Him?

Prayer

Father God, You are awesome and we want You to fit into the biggest box You make in heaven—none of these little engagement-ring boxes.

Sometimes we feel like You have left us to ourselves, but we know better than that. Give us the heavenly wisdom to recognize that You are doing a godly work in us. We continue to submit to Your will for our lives. When we feel like screaming and rebelling at You, may we remember that You are truly on our team.

We thank You for all the good things You have given us, and may we accept the hard character-building traits that are part of our training. Amen.

Taking Action

- In your journal list those areas in your life where God has done a new work in you.

- List those areas that are in process of change.

- List those areas which haven't been given to Him yet, but which are about to be placed in His hands.

- As a couple, make again a reconfirming commitment that you want God to do a good work in you.

Reading On

1 Corinthians 10:13   Romans 8:28
Romans 4:20,21   John 10:10

Happiness Is . . .

Scripture Reading: Psalm 1:1-6

Key Verses: Psalm 1:1-3

> *Blessed is the man who does not walk in the counsel of the wicked or stand in the way of sinners or sit in the seat of mockers. But his delight is in the law of the Lord, and on his law he meditates day and night. He is like a tree planted by streams of water, which yields its fruit in season and whose leaf does not wither. Whatever he does prospers.*

Eight men were once traveling together, and each related his experience in reply to the question "Are you fully happy?" A banker said he had acquired a fortune, which was invested securely; he had a lovely and devoted family, yet the thought that he must leave them all forever cast a funeral pall over the declining years of his life.

A military officer said he had known glory and the intoxication of triumph; but after the battle he passed over the field and found a brother officer dying. He tried to relieve him, but the dying man said, "Thank you, but it's too late. We must all die; think about it, think about it." This scene gripped the officer, and he could find no deliverance from it. So he confessed his unhappiness.

A diplomat spoke of the honors and gratitude showered upon him during a long and successful career, yet confessed an emptiness of the heart, a secret malady which all his honors could not cure.

A poet told of the pleasures he enjoyed with the muses; of the applause of the people; of his fame, which he was assured was immortal. But, dissatisfied, he cried out, "What is such an immortality?" and declared his unsatisfied longing for a higher immortality.

A man of the world said that his effort had been to laugh at everything—to look at the bright side of things and be happy; to find pleasure in the ballroom, theater, and other amusements; yet he confessed that he was sometimes melancholy, and was far from perfectly happy.

A lawyer said he had health, wealth, reputation, and a good marriage, and that during his career he longed for just what he now possessed; but he did not find the expected enjoyment in it, and contentment was not his heritage. His hours were long and his existence monotonous; he was not fully happy.

A religious professor, a ritualist, professed his strict adherence to the doctrines of the gospel and his punctual performance of religious duties, without being happy at all.

A Christian physician related his vain search for happiness in the world and in his profession; but then he had been led by Scripture to see himself a sinner and to look to Christ as his Savior. Since that time he found peace, contentment, and joy, and had no fear of the end, which to him was only the beginning.

One of a couple's true quests of life is learning how to be happy. Everywhere we look, people are searching for their happiness by the job they have, the homes they live in, the toys they play with, the food they eat, and the vacations they take. At the end of each of these things we are supposed to find this magic thing called happiness. But to our amazement, when we finally arrive at this great destination we often find that happiness has moved and left no forwarding address.

A poet once said, "Happiness is much more equally divided than some of us imagine. One man shall possess most of the materials but little of the thing; another man possesses much of the thing but very few of the materials."

This tension is one of life's greatest struggles: How do we balance between things and happiness? In today's passage we concentrate on three areas of this profile:

- What to avoid
- What to concentrate on
- What a happy person is like

What to Avoid

David warns us not to take advice from the wrong people. Paul likewise in Romans 3:4 states, "Let God be true and every man a liar." The world system is trying to whittle away at our value system and make us conform to the world's way of thinking. As a couple, be true to each other and seek wise counsel. The magazines, television, radio, and movies don't speak with godly wisdom. (It's amazing how often I hear people express how they came to a certain conclusion at a fork in the road of life!) Turn to Scripture instead, plus wise Christian counsel. This passage also tells us not to go along with what sinners do or to hang around those who criticize and make fun of others.

The bottom line is to have quality friends—friends that have good character qualities and can provide good wisdom in their speech.

What to Concentrate On

Psalm 1:2 says we are to delight in the law of the Lord and to meditate on His law day and night. Concentration is one area of life that we have difficulty accomplishing. We have become so brainwashed by our media that all episodes of life are narrowed to a 30-minute time slot. Our evening news readers give sound bites to the event, usually highlighting those bites to reinforce the political persuasion of the station.

Two areas of emphasis are to delight and meditate. Do we find ourselves going to Scripture with delight, and are we able to chew on it all day long? If we would approach Scripture each day in this way we would see wonderful changes take place in our lives. Our families would be changed, along with our churches, communities, and nation.

What a Happy Person is Like

David writes in verse three that our lives can become like a tree that is firmly planted in a place where there is a lot of water and that has leaves which stay fresh and green even in the heat and fruit which grows abundantly.

What kind of tree are you today?

- I'm a young tree, growing but not real established.
- My leaves tend to dry up in times of heat and stress.
- I'm a tree with no leaves and no fruit.
- I thought my roots were pretty deep but a recent storm nearly blew me over.
- I'm seeing more and more good fruit appear in my life.
- I wish I had more leaves to protect people from the heat.
- I'm like a tree that's just a little too far away from the water, feeling a little dry.

The Christian doctor in our opening story shared that he had been led by Scripture to see himself as a sinner and to look to Christ as his Savior; since that time he found peace, contentment, and joy, and had no fear of the end, which to him was but the beginning.

Prayer

Father God, as a couple we want to be happy in the Lord. We earnestly desire to have a balance between the things of life and a desire to be anchored to You by planting our trees by the streams of water so that we can yield fruit in season. We want our leaves to be healthy and not to wither during the hot seasons of life. Bring us into fellowship with godly couples—those who can build us up in the Lord. We give You relationships and want You to guide us into right friendships. Amen.

Taking Action

- As a couple evaluate your friends. Are they helpful or harmful to you as a couple?

- Continue to solidify those relationships which build you up and gradually separate yourselves from unhealthy relationships.

- Individually write in your journal an accurate description of the kind of tree that your life is like right now.

- What changes can be made to make your tree healthier?

Reading On

Galatians 5:22,23
Matthew 7:13,14
1 John 5:12

We don't become holy by acquiring merit badges and Brownie points. It has nothing to do with virtue or job descriptions or morality. It is nothing we can do, in this do-it-yourself world. It is a gift, sheer gift, waiting there to be recognized and received. We do not have to be qualified to be holy.

—*Madeleine L'Engle*

A Discerning Heart

Scripture Reading: 1 Kings 3:5-15

Key Verse: 1 Kings 3:9

> *Give your servant a discerning heart to gov-*
> *ern your people and to distinguish between*
> *right and wrong.*

———————— ✆ ————————

An English theologian tells the story of a young man who went to college. When he had been there a year his father asked him, "What do you know? Do you know more than when you went?" "Oh, yes!" he replied, "I do."

Then he went the second year, and was asked the same question: "Do you know more than when you went?" "Oh, no!" he replied; "I know a great deal less." "Well," said the father, "you are making progress."

Then he went the third year, and was asked, "What do you know now?" "Oh!" he replied, "I don't think I know anything." "That's right," said the father; "you have now learned to profit, since you say you know nothing."

He who is convinced that he knows nothing of him-self as he ought to know gives up steering his ship and lets God put his hand on the rudder. He lays aside his own wisdom and cries out, "O God, my little wisdom is cast at Your feet; my little judgment is given to You."

Solomon must have been similar to this young college

student, for he too knew the wisdom of being humble when it came to leading the people he had inherited from his father, King David. In his dream from today's passage, God asked Solomon, "Ask for whatever you want me to give you." Solomon in all of his youth (about 20 years old) declared with great wisdom, "Give your servant a discerning heart to govern your people and to distinguish between right and wrong. For who is able to govern this great people of yours?"

What a great declaration to know that by his own power he wasn't qualified to lead and to govern his people! He also wanted to know right from wrong.

Mom and Dad, do you hear the simple humility of such a great man of God? If he didn't feel confident in that task, is it any wonder that sometimes we are dismayed at trying to lead our children properly? If Solomon could so humbly face God and ask Him such a simple request, why should we feel at a loss when we too feel helpless?

As parents we need to be up front when it comes to asking for discernment from God. Notice also that Solomon started his request with this statement about himself: "So give your servant . . . ." We need to approach God as a servant, one who realizes that only through the power and guidance from God can he do anything. We aren't capable under our own strength.

Throughout this complete passage in 1 Kings we see that Solomon recognized:

- who God was;
- who Solomon was;
- his own responsibility to God.

These are the same three recognitions that we must make:

- who God is;
- who we are;
- what our responsibilities are to God.

We have a very big God. He is bigger than anything in our past, anything in the future, and bigger than any box. Yes, we serve a very big God.

Also note in 1 Kings 3:10-15 the blessings that Solomon received even though he did not ask for them:

- riches
- honor
- long life

As long as we are in God's will, He will give us far more than we have asked for in our prayers. Oh, to have that kind of faith! As a couple can we believe that God loves us so much that He will more than meet our every provision?

Prayer

Father God, may we as a couple approach Your throne with us being Your servants. As a family we want to serve You in our marriage, family, church, community, and work. When our egos get involved, remind us that we are truly Your servants and want to do Your will, not ours.

Both of us pray for discerning hearts and to know right from wrong. Thank You for this new dimension You have shared with us today. Amen.

Taking Action

- Discuss with your mate how you each can have more of a servant's heart.

- Is there any discernment that either Mom or Dad has regarding his or her marriage? Their children?

- Express verbally to each other what today's lesson meant to you.

Reading On

1 Chronicles 29:1
Ephesians 6:18

A Child's Heart and a
Grown-Up Head

Christ never meant that we were to remain children in intelligence; on the contrary, He told us to be not only "as harmless as doves" but also "as wise as serpents." He wants a child's heart, but a grown-up's head. He wants us to be simple, single-minded, affectionate, and teachable, as good children are; but He also wants every bit of intelligence we have to be alert at its job, and in first-class fighting trim.

—*C.S. Lewis*

A Letter from a Friend

Scripture Reading: Psalm 23:1-6

Key Verse: Psalm 23:6

> *Surely goodness and love will follow me all the days of my life, and I will dwell in the house of the Lord forever.*

Dear Friend:

I just had to send a note to tell you how much I love you and care about you. I saw you yesterday as you were walking with your friends. I waited all day hoping you would want to talk with me also. As evening drew near, I gave you a sunset to close your day and a cool breeze to rest you. And I waited. But you never came. It hurt me, but I still love you because I am your friend.

I saw you fall asleep last night and I longed to touch your brow. So I spilled moonlight on your pillow and your face. Again I waited, wanting to rush down so we could talk. I have so many gifts for you. But you awakened late the next day and rushed back to work. My tears were in the rain.

Today you looked so sad, so all alone. It makes my heart ache because I understand. My friends let me down and hurt me so many times too. But I love you. Oh, if you would only listen to me. I really love you. I try to tell you in the blue sky and in the quiet green grass. I whisper it in the leaves on the trees and breathe it in the colors of the flowers. I shout it to you in the mountain streams and give the birds love songs to sing. I clothe you with warm sunshine and perfume the air with nature's scents. My love for you is deeper than the oceans and bigger than the biggest want or need in your heart.

If you only knew how much I want to help you. I want you to meet my Father. He wants to help you, too. My Father is that way, you know. Just call me, ask me, talk with me. I have so much to share with you. Yet I won't hassle you. I'll wait because I love you.

Your Friend,
Jesus[4]

What a great truth to know that God actually loves and cares for me! I had a difficult time realizing that God would have died on the cross just for me and my sins.

As a couple, we don't want to have Jesus wait for our stubbornness before we relinquish control of our lives and tell Him that we love Him too.

Jesus must have a lot of patience to wait for us. I'm sure He longs and cries for our repentance, but we just go along living our own selfish lives, doing our own thing—whatever that thing might be.

Campus Crusade provides a very simple little booklet which outlines four principles that will help you discover how to know God personally and experience the abundant life he promised in John 10:10:

1. God loves you and created you to know Him personally (John 3:16; John 17:3).

2. Man is sinful and separated from God, so we can not know Him personally or experience His love (Romans 3:23; 6:23).

3. Jesus Christ is God's only provision for man's sin. Through Him alone we can know God personally and experience His love (Romans 5:8; 1 Corinthians 15:3-6; John 14:6).

4. We must individually receive Jesus Christ as Savior and Lord; then we can know God personally and experience His love (John 1:12; Ephesians 2:8-9, John 3:1-8; Revelation 3:20).

You can receive Christ right now by faith through this suggested prayer:

> *Lord Jesus, I want to know You personally. Thank You for dying on the cross for my sins. I open the door of my life and receive You as my Savior and Lord. Thank You for forgiving my sins and giving me eternal life. Take control of the throne of my life. Make me the kind of person You want me to be. Amen.* [5]

Taking Action

- Does this prayer express the desire of your heart?
- According to Revelation 3:20, where is Christ right now in relation to you?

- On what authority do you know that God has answered your prayer? Read 1 John 5:11-13 and Hebrews 13:5.

- Share this decision with your spouse, a friend, someone at work, etc.

- If you have already accepted Christ as your personal Savior, pause and give thanks to Him for all He has done for you in the past, the present, and the future.

- As a couple become more committed as fellow believers.

Reading On

Read all the verses of Scripture that have been given to support these four principles of salvation.

The Righteous Will Live by Faith

Scripture Reading: Galatians 3:10–4:11

Key Verse: Galatians 3:11

Clearly no one is justified before God by the law, because "The righteous will live by faith."

———— ⟨ॐ⟩ ————

When the first suspension bridge across the Niagara River was to be erected, the question was how to get the cable across the river. With a favoring wind a kite was sent aloft, which soon landed on the other shore. To its thin string a larger cord was attached, which was drawn over the river—then a rope, then a larger rope, then a cable strong enough to support the iron cable which in turn supported the bridge.

All of this could never have been done without the thin kitestring. Even so, a weak faith reaches to Christ and heaven, and may enlarge to gigantic proportions, and holding its possessor securely anchored within the veil.

That's the way we are as a couple. Our faith starts as an insignificant string and then develops into a cord, then a rope, then a large rope, and finally a cable. In our world of comparisons we want to start out right away as a cable because that's what we see around us. But always remember that those cables started out as insignificant strings and have developed and grown over the years into that cable you so greatly admire today.

Spiritual growth results from trusting in God the Father, God the Son, and God the Holy Spirit. In today's key verse we see that the righteous man (or woman) lives by faith. That faith must have an object, and for the Christian that Object is Jesus Christ. He was given to us as believers to atone for our sins; through Him we have forgiveness of those sins and a direct line to God the Father.

A life of faith will enable you as a couple to trust God increasingly with every detail of your life, and to practice the following:

G — Go to God in daily prayer (John 15:7).

R — Read God's Word daily (Acts 17:11).
Begin with the Gospel of John.

O — Obey God moment by moment (John 14:21).

W — Witness for Christ by your life and words (Matthew 4:19; John 15:8).

T — Trust God for every detail of your life (1 Peter 5:7).

H — Holy Spirit: Allow Him to control and empower your daily life and witness (Galatians 5:16,17; Acts 1:8).

Growth as a Christian is a matter of choice. Each day you must make that crucial decision again: Am I going to follow Jesus today? Each day you must gather from your soul the answer, "Yes, I am going to follow Jesus today!" You might be thinking, "Do I have to make this same decision every day for the rest of my life?" Our answer to you is, "Yes, you have to make this same fundamental decision each day." The fruits and blessings of today are based upon the decisions you made yesterday. Success generally doesn't come by accident. Develop a plan and let the plan work for you.

Prayer

Father God, as we meet You today in prayer, we want to grow in our Christian walk. Sometimes we get discouraged by all of life's perils. We work long hours, drive a long way each day to work, face extreme pressures at work, and then head for home with another segment of our lives to deal with—our home and children.

We pray that You will help us stay focused on what's important. Let us have the ability to prioritize what's important and what's not.

Thank You for making us as ordinary people (insignificant strings) to want to grow into giant cables. Establish our feet into proper motion and direction. Make us want to say yes to this basic question of life, for we want to be pleasing to Your desires for us. Amen.

Taking Action

- Go through the Scripture verses for GROWTH.

- Discuss the contents with your mate.

- List a few areas of your life that need growth. What are you going to do to strengthen these areas?

- Thank God for what He is going to do in your life.

Reading On

Hebrews 11:1-39
Matthew 17:20

What Are Your Priorities?

Scripture Reading: Jeremiah 9:23, 24

Key Verse: Jeremiah 9:23

> *This is what the Lord says: "Let not the wise man boast of his wisdom or the strong man boast of his strength or the rich man boast of his riches."*

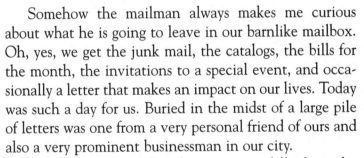

Somehow the mailman always makes me curious about what he is going to leave in our barnlike mailbox. Oh, yes, we get the junk mail, the catalogs, the bills for the month, the invitations to a special event, and occasionally a letter that makes an impact on our lives. Today was such a day for us. Buried in the midst of a large pile of letters was one from a very personal friend of ours and also a very prominent businessman in our city.

As I opened it and took it very carefully from the business envelope, I began to read:

Dear Friend and Olsan's customer:

What do you do when you make a major change in your business, move and build new offices so you can be closer to your customers, and then find out that it doesn't take you back to the fun of 20 or 30 years ago in your career, and that what you are doing now is really no longer your life goal . . . in fact, is really contrary to what is now important in life? I realize the only answer is to share my thoughts and ask your understanding.

I have decided to close the store and retire.

I am so very proud of our company and its position in the Inland Empire. No employer could ask for a finer bunch of people than our employees, who have given their hearts in trying to establish and maintain the professional standards we have set for ourselves and endeavored to live by. We have laughed, cried, and worked very hard together to accomplish our mission. I salute them, and thank them for allowing me to share part of my life with such a fine group!

This is a fast-paced and ever-changing world we live in, and retailing is no different. The furniture industry is going through a huge change on a national basis, and I am sure these changes ultimately will offer the public some new choices, which is good. As a business person, I must decide on the priorities, goals, and standards I am going to live and do business by, and then decide the very difficult question if I am willing to pay the price to continue a successful career.

I have never felt that I have been able to give my family the attention and energy they deserve and I desire, and I can't see that it is going to get any better . . . even though I always dreamed it would. The changes in retailing are most certainly not going to allow for *more* personal time! My priorities have changed. The decision was not an easy one to make, but one that will be right for me and my family.

Thank you for your attention and understanding.

Harvey B. Olsan

As I finished reading this letter my heart was touched by its sincerity and Harvey's concern for his longtime employees and customers. But I had a greater concern for Harvey and his family. Here was a man who stood tall in the saddle and was able to say, "What you are doing now is really no longer your life goal . . . in fact, is really contrary to what is now important in life."

This is a man who has the courage to admit to himself that after 51 years of working in a family business he no longer wants to continue the sacrifices to keep it afloat.

How many of us out there are in the same situation? Be willing to recognize that goals of the past are no longer goals of the future. It's okay to change direction in life. Maybe you and your spouse need to come together and rewrite your purpose in life. It's okay, it's not carved in granite. Don't get caught up in the unimportant things of life. Concentrate on those things that will matter 20 years from now—your family. What good does it do a man to gain the whole world but lose his own family?

Major on the major things of life. Break yourself away from the minor things you think are major but really aren't.

Prayer

> *Father God, as a family we truly want to discern those areas of our life which are important. Let us be free from spending so much energy, time, and money on things that aren't important. Today's lesson has given us confirmation that a family can change life-long priorities. Thanks for revealing to me that some things are more important in life than other things. It's okay to change. I appreciate that insight. May we as a couple have godly discernment to focus our lives on the most important things. Amen.*

Taking Action

- Sit down with your mate and reconfirm the direction of your lives.

- List five things that are truly positive aspects in your life and five things that don't seem to be getting you where you want to go.

- Praise God for the five pluses, and then spend time on the five negatives to find new direction in these areas.

- Set a date on your calendar three months from now to review your progress.

- Be willing to rewrite some goals that need to be changed. What might they be? List three. What can you do to change each of these?

Reading On

Psalm 127:3-5
Matthew 18:1-6

You are in my heart forever and I live and die with you. I have the highest confidence in you, and my pride in you is great.

—2 Corinthians 7:3,4 TLB

Refined by Fire

Scripture Reading: Job 23:1-12
Key Verse: Job 23:10

He knows the way that I take; when he has tested me, I will come forth as gold.

——————— ✍ ———————

I stopped on my way downstairs last night to speak to Jennie, who had just gone to bed in her cozy little room. I bent over to kiss her. "Jennie," I asked, "do you love Jesus?" "Oh, yes!" she replied. "Are you sure? How do you know?" "Why, of course I know," she said. "Don't I feel it all over inside?" "That's good!" I thought. "I wish everyone had that same consciousness of love; there wouldn't be so many fearful Christians.

"Do you think Jesus knows that you love Him, Jennie?" "Why, of course!" she answered again. "Doesn't He know everything? Doesn't He look right down into my heart and see the love there?" "Well, Jennie," I continued, "How can I know it? I can't look into your heart."

Jennie sprang to her feet. On the wall at the side of her bed hung a large picture sheet containing 12 scenes in the life of Christ; a number of short texts were printed here and there around the border. Putting her tiny fingers on one of these, without speaking she turned around and looked triumphantly up into my face. I turned on the

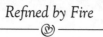

light, and read, "If ye love me, keep my command-ments."[6]

When pain comes into our lives it's so easy to ask "Why, Lord?" Why, Lord, do the righteous suffer?

If there ever was a man who loved and obeyed God, it was Job. Yet his testing was very dramatic and ex-tremely painful. Today all we have to do is pick up a newspaper in any part of the world and read of tragedy touching both the just and the unjust.

Our friends Glen and Marilyn Heavilin have lost three sons prematurely: one to crib death, one twin, Ethan, to pneumonia as an infant, then the second twin, Nathan, as a teenager to a drunk driver. Were Glen and Marilyn tested? You bet! Did they come forth as gold? You bet! Today they use their experiences to glorify the name of the Lord.

Marilyn has written five books. Her first, *Roses in De-cember,*[7] tells the story of their great loss. Marilyn has had the opportunity to speak all over the country in high school auditoriums filled with teenagers. There she shares her story and has the platform to talk about life and death, chemical dependency, and God Himself.

Did God know what He was doing when He chose the Heavilins? Of course. They have come forth as gold fired in the heat of life and polished to shine for Him. Is their pain gone? Never. Can they go forth to minister? Absolutely. They have been very active in a group called "Compassionate Friends," which supports families who have experienced the death of a child. I thank God for Christians like the Heavilins. God knew the path they would take when tragedy came into their lives.

Everyone has experienced some kind of tragedy. How we handle these events is crucial. Today there are many

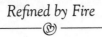
wonderful support groups available in churches and local communities.

I grew up with a violent, alcoholic father. I had no place to go and no one to talk to, so I stuffed my pain. Now there are several groups to help people who find themselves in situations like mine.

A church in Southern California has a large group that meets weekly and has become like a church within a church for those who are chemically dependent, as well as for their families. Lives have changed as they pray for each other, support each other, and cry together. Many people are coming forth as gold.

Bob and I visited a church in Memphis, Tennessee, which had a support group for homosexuals. Because of this church's outreach, many were coming out of the gay lifestyle and coming forth as gold.

Whatever your test is today, please know that others have experienced and are experiencing your pain. Don't go through the testing alone. Contact the local church and find another person with whom you can share and cry. You too can come forth as gold.

Jesus knows and has experienced our pain. He is always with us to help us get through the tough times in life. Trust Him now. It's all part of the coming forth as gold that Job talks about.

Prayer

Father God, it is hard to desire testing in order to be more Christlike. However, I know from experience that we rarely grow in good times. It's the intense heat that makes us pure. May I be gold and not wood, hay, or stubble. Amen.

Taking Action

- Write down in your journal what pain and/or test you are experiencing today.

- Take a step to help yourself work toward becoming as gold.

- Write a letter to God about how you feel.

- Get involved in a support group.

Reading On

Psalm 66:10   2 Corinthians 4:7-9
Psalm 51:10

Prayer pushes the light and hope
into dark corners of your life.

Praying Parents

Scripture Reading: James 5:13-18

Key Verse: James 5:16

> *Confess your sins to each other and pray for each other so that you may be healed. The prayer of a righteous man is powerful and effective.*

"Oh, Mom and Dad, I'm off to school. I've got to run and catch the bus. Fridays are big days and today is no exception. Pray for me. I've got a big test in physics and advanced English studies. Thanks, see you tonight. Have a good day, God bless."

Quick, short, and to the point! Very similar to many of our rush-rush lives: always running late, never enough time. However, in this short goodbye speech we observe a very special quality: prayer. It is obvious that the child and parents are used to supporting each other in prayer.

As parents we don't want to wait until it's too late to start praying in our family life. Unprotected children are very vulnerable to Satan's attack. The greatest shield of protection that we as parents can provide for our children is prayer.

If we wait until the children are older, then we become desperate and are left with "crisis praying."

"Devote yourselves to prayer, being watchful and thankful" (Colossians 4:2).

It is clear through this passage that we are to be—

- devoted to prayer
- watchful
- thankful.

Prayer builds a hedge around those you pray for. Without this protection those we love go out into the world unprotected. If we are to be watchful, evidently there is something out there to watch. If we aren't aware of danger it might very easily engulf us and harm us. Prayer also gives us a thankful heart for all the things the Lord gives to us.

As a couple, today become devoted in prayer for your children, no matter how old they are.

Campus Crusade through their radio ministry "Family Life Today" gives us parents seven tips for prayerful parents.

SPECIFICS TO PRAY ABOUT

1. That God would place a protective hedge around our children so strong that Satan cannot enter and lead them into temptation (Psalm 33:20; James 5:8).

2. That children would use godly wisdom in selecting their friends, for friends and peers do make a difference (Proverbs 1:10; Deuteronomy 13:6,8). Ask God to give our children a discernment of people as well as knowing the difference between right and wrong.

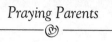
3. That our children would stay pure (Psalm 24:4; Job 17:9).

4. They will be caught if they wander into cheating, lies, or mischief (Proverbs 20:30).

5. That they will be alert and thinking clearly as they attend school and take exams and they will be motivated to do the best they are capable of doing (Ephesians 4:1).

6. For the spouses that your children will one day marry: that they will come from godly homes and will have an appetite for spiritual truth; that their goals and purposes will be the same as those of your own children, and that their future homes would be characterized by Deuteronomy 5:29: "They [would have] such a heart in them that they would fear Me and keep all My commandments always" (NASB).

7. That our children's lives will count for God and that He will use them as a testimony and witness for His glory. Ask that they exceed us, not materially or educationally, but in their spiritual walk (Psalm 103:17,18; Isaiah 54:13; Psalm 78:1-8).[8]

Prayer

Father God, thank You for giving us the desire to pray for our children and/or grandchildren. May we remain faithful in this discipline. We certainly can appreciate our children's need to be shielded by this hedge of protection at home, school, church, and leisure activities. Amen.

Taking Action

- Begin today to pray specifically for your children.

- Pray for specific number one on Sunday, number two on Monday, number three on Tuesday, and so on.

- Write your children an occasional note and let them know that you specifically prayed for them today.

- Let them know verbally that you are praying for their protection.

Reading On

Go through the Scripture that is given to support each prayer topic.

Endurance and Encouragement

Scripture Reading: Romans 15:1-13

Key Verse: Romans 15:4

> *Everything that was written in the past was written to teach us, so that through endurance and the encouragement of the Scriptures we might have hope.*

We live in a consumer world that is always asking questions that relate to how much endurance:

- When we go to buy something we ask, "How long will it last?"

- The personnel manager at work wants to know how long you will be with the company. Are you here for the long haul?

- In marriage we want our partner to be committed forever. How long is our marriage going to last?

- In athletics endurance is very important. The coach asks, "Are you in shape to play a complete game and for 140 games of the season?"

- God also wants to know if you are into faith for the duration.

In today's passages we see that through reading the Scriptures we are taught to have endurance and encouragement and ultimately hope. Oh, do we as a couple ever need to have these three qualities in our Christian experience! Can you imagine joining a club, association, or league without knowing the rules? How many times has an insurance agent advised you of a privilege that his or her company offers that you never knew of before? What a thrill to learn something new, particularly when it is to our advantage!

Scripture is the same way: We read it and marvel at the new revelation. That's one reason why each of us needs to be in God's Word daily. We are always coming across new mysteries and revelations that we never knew before.

Get into the habit of daily reading Scripture because you want to, not because someone tells you to. Self-motivation is the best reason to do something.

Paul writes in 2 Timothy 3:16,17, "All Scripture is God-breathed and is useful for teaching, rebuking, correcting, and training in righteousness, so that the man of God may be thoroughly equipped for every good work."

As you and your mate read Romans 15:1-13 today, you may feel defeated, having little endurance, encouragement, and hope. You may have almost given up the faith and be tempted to fall back to your old ways, your old friends, and your old habits. May we be an encouragement to you and renew that spark of your first love for Christ!

In verse 13 of this Scripture passage we read, "May the God of hope fill you with all joy and peace as you trust in him, so that you may overflow with hope by the power of the Holy Spirit."

Only through the power of the Holy Spirit are we able to make this transition. If we try it with human effort we will become discouraged and defeated.

Begin anew today. Be lifted up through Christ, even as He was lifted up on the cross for our sins.

Prayer

> *Father God, we truly want to exhibit the eternal hope that You speak about in Scripture for our lives. You know we don't want to live defeated lives. Give us a newness of heart. Refresh our souls, and may we again capture the freshness of a new beginning. Today let us touch another person's life with Your sweet fragrance. Amen.*

Taking Action

- Ask God today for new endurance, encouragement, and hope.
- Share this decision with a fellow believer. Ask him or her to hold you accountable this month.
- Seek out someone—a family member, a neighbor, someone at work, a casual meeting of a person in line at the market—and be an encouragement to him or her.

Reading On

Psalm 69:9   Romans 4:21

Daily Couple Affirmation

- God has good plans for us today that give us both a future and a hope.
  —*From Jeremiah 29:11*

- God is the blessed controller of all things today.
  — *From 1 Timothy 6:15*

- We are foreordained to be molded into the image of His Son, Jesus, today.
  —*From Romans 8:29*

- We can do all things through Christ, who strengthens us today.
  —*From Philippians 4:13*

- We are responsible to bear much fruit today, and thereby glorify the Father.
  —*From John 15:8*

- Nothing can separate us from the love of Christ today.
  —*From Romans 8:35,38,39*

- God is the love of our lives, and He has called us in accordance with His purpose; therefore He has promised us that all things will work together today for our good.
  —*From Romans 8:28*

- God loves us with an everlasting love today.
  —*From Jeremiah 31:3*

If My People Pray

Scripture Reading: 2 Chronicles 7:12-22
Key Verse: 2 Chronicles 7:14

> *If my people, who are called by my name, will humble themselves and pray and seek my face and turn from their wicked ways, then will I hear from heaven and will forgive their sin and will heal their land.*

A poor Macedonian soldier was leading before Alexander the Great a mule laden with gold for the king's use. The mule became so tired that he could no longer carry the load, so the mule driver took it off and carried it himself, with great difficulty, for a considerable distance. Finally Alexander saw him sinking under the burden and about to throw it to the ground, so he cried out, "Friend, do not be weary yet; try to carry it to your tent, for it is now all yours!"

This blessing is much better than the lottery. Who says, "Good guys finish last!" Humility certainly has its blessings. Ezra, the writer of 1 and 2 Chronicles, certainly knew the importance of humility because he directed this passage to his people, people who God called by name.

He states that in order for God's people to receive His blessings there are four basic requirements:

- humility
- prayer
- devotion
- repentance

This is an appropriate prayer for all of America, Christian and non-Christian alike. We shake our heads with disbelief at the depravity of man. Each day the headlines in the newspaper scream out stabbings, shootings, murder, drunkenness, rape, and incest. Where have we gone wrong as a nation? Are we losing those qualities that have made America strong? Are our families breaking apart along with the moral fiber of this country? How can we get back on track to recapture the greatness of the past?

In 450 B.C. Ezra wrote to his people the words found in verse 14 for today.

He says we are to humble ourselves, to pray, to seek God's face, and to repent of our sins. Then God will—

- answer our prayers;
- forgive our sins; and
- heal our land.

As a couple may you recognize the truths of this passage and come to God with all humility, committing each of your lives again to the righteousness of God. Vow that in your home you will make a difference. No longer will you go along with the tide of the country. You and your family will say, "Stop, no more, let's return to the timeless principles that are written in the Bible."

Remember what Susanna Wesley said about the gospel:

- We believe it;
- We live it.

We need couples who will not only believe the Bible but will begin to live it. Start today in your own family to live it.

Prayer

Father God, You know how we long to return America to the virtues that made this country great. Change will come about through changed families, and we want to sign up as one of those team members to change the downhill direction of our country. Sometimes it seems like such an awesome task, but we trust that You will give us the necessary conviction, energy, love, and passion to make a small dent through Your ways of goodness.

May each member of our family be excited about this new beginning! Amen.

Taking Action

- Write today's key verse in your journal and underline it in your Bible (date the margin).
- Come together as a family at mealtime and discuss this challenge.

- Ask the total family how you can live out this challenge in day-to-day living.
- Pray jointly for our country and our families.

Reading On

2 Chronicles 6:37-39   James 4:10

Spring/Summer Fall/Winter

Scripture Reading: Ecclesiastes 3:1-11

Key Verses: Ecclesiastes 3:1,2

> *There is a time for everything, and a season for every activity under heaven . . . a time to plant and a time to uproot.*

———— ⊛ ————

Throughout the *Farmer's Almanac* we read detailed descriptions about planting, reaping, and harvesting— when to plant and when to rest. The fruits of sowing our seeds are based not only on what we do but on the elements of nature. We must be prepared to do all we can and then be willing to let God do the rest.

SPRING

In the springtime of life we plant our seeds. We are so excited about all the newness of life: courtship, a wedding, a new job, children, a new home, and all the rest of the excitements that come along with spring. We are full of all the hope and anticipation of what life has to offer. Many times we are naive about what we are doing. Unless we really have it together as a couple, we give little thought or reason to why we do what we do.

A tried and true farmer isn't quite as nonchalant about this season of life. He realizes that in order to have a good harvest he must have a good spring. He must know what crop he is planting, make proper seed selection, plant after the last frost, and pray that rain or irrigation comes at the proper time.

Spring is crucial in life because what happens in these three months greatly affects what the remaining three seasons of the year will be like.

We too as a couple must take the proper care to realize that the seeds we plant in the early part of our lives determines what the rest of our lives will be.

Establish your life goals and purposes during this phase of your life. Be patient and be willing to postpone your desires for instant gratification.

One of our mottos is: "Success is progressive realization of worthwhile goals." Spring is the time of life when we begin to establish these goals.

SUMMER

Many times the drudgery of summer makes us lose sight of what life is all about. During these long, hot days we must press on and remember why we are on this earth. It isn't by accident that we are here. Occasionally we will have a thunderstorm to break the monotony of this period of life.

This is also true of our marriage. We must hoe out the weeds of life that attempt to snuff out the young plants as they stick their heads out of the soil.

Spring is the freshness of newness, but summer tests us to see if we really have the discipline and godly character to see life through these difficult periods. Many would-be farmers and would-be marriages never get through this phase of life. Only those with dedicated and serious purpose survive. Life often gets boring during this season, but we must always remember that in order to get to the harvest season, we must get through the summer.

Your marriage will receive the maximum tensions during summer, so continue to reaffirm your commitment and purpose to each other. In Genesis 2:24 we read, "A man will leave his father and mother and be united to his wife, and they will become one flesh." Summer is when we become one and continue to pledge to our mate that we have one purpose.

FALL

Now fall is here—all what we have worked for so long and so hard. At last we will be able to reap the harvest of our efforts—if we have done a good job in spring and summer.

"Whoever sows sparingly will also reap sparingly, and whoever sows generously will also reap generously" (2 Corinthians 9:7).

This is the season of life where we receive our blessings. In order to have abundance, we must have sowed with abundance. This is our pay period of life. In Proverbs 24:3,4 we are promised that our rooms will be filled with rare and beautiful riches.

These rare and beautiful riches are our children, friends, good health, emotional and psychological stability, and above all our love for the Lord—just the things we hoped for when we were in the springtime of life.

One of the warnings of this season is not to use up all of our harvest. We must save some seeds and fruits so that we will have something to plant next spring. There will be another spring, and we certainly want to be prepared when it comes.

As grandparents we certainly see the importance of saving for the next spring—not only for ours, but for those of our inheritance. After all, we are raising more than one generation.

WINTER

At last winter has arrived and we can have a more relaxed and easy pace around the farm. Much of the day is cool, the land is frozen, and icy wind is blowing from the plains of the north. The wife and I can spend rich times in conversing, looking back over life with some smiles and some frowns, but generally pleased about the accomplishments of spring, summer, and fall. A good book, a CD of soft music, a nap in the afternoon, an early dinner, and off to a good night's sleep.

Isn't it cozy with just the two of us around the fireplace? We can look each other in the eyes and say, "God bless and good night—you are truly my best friend!"

Enjoy winter—it's so rejuvenating!

Prayer

Father God, thank You for the seasons of life. May we realize that we must be good stewards of our seasons. Let us grasp the awesomeness of this concept. May we enjoy each season and reap the blessings that each offer. Thank You for planting into us a desire to follow You and Your principles for a rich, rewarding, and meaningful life. Thank You for giving us a plan and purpose. Amen.

Taking Action

- In which season of life do you find yourself?
- What goals and purposes have you established for this season?
- What do you want fall to look like?
- What are you doing to accomplish the fall look?

Reading On

Proverbs 24:3,4
Matthew 6:33

We Are Not Alone

We need to feel more to understand others.

We need to love more to be loved back.

We need to cry more to cleanse ourselves.

We need to laugh more to enjoy ourselves.

We need to see more other than our own little fantasies.

We need to hear more and listen to the needs of others.

We need to give more and take less.

We need to share more and own less.

We need to look more and realize that we are not so different from one another.

We need to create a world where all can peacefully live the life they choose.

—*Susan Polis Schutz*

Who We Are in God

Scripture Reading: Psalm 27:1-14

Key Verses: Psalm 27:7,8

> *Hear my voice when I call, O Lord; be merciful to me and answer me. My heart says of you, "Seek his face!" Your face, Lord, I will seek.*

———————⟨☙⟩———————

One of the great truths of Scripture is to find out who we are in God—not our stature in life, not our wealth, not our material possessions, not our physical appearance, but who we are in God.

In the above anthem of praise, David expresses his confidence in the Lord (verses 1-6), prays for continued victory (verses 7-12), and rejoices in his waiting on the Lord (verses 13,14).

It is said in Scripture that David was a man after God's own heart. He was considered a truly godly man.

In this passage we can select words that answer four basic questions about God and His presence in our lives:

- Who God is
- What God does
- Who we are
- What we do

Who God Is

- He is our Lord
- He is our salvation
- He is good
- He is our defense of life
- He is light
- He is a teacher
- He is my Savior
- He is beauty

What God Does

- He defends us
- He keeps us safe
- He will hide me
- He lifts us up
- He protects us from false witness
- He hears my voice
- He receives us unconditionally
- He is sovereign
- He puts us above circumstances

Who We Are

- We are worshipers
- We seek God
- We are insecure because we do not ask
- We have enemies
- We need leadership
- We are impatient
- We experience rejection
- We are fearful
- We are learners
- We are God's child
- We are servants of God
- We are petitioners in prayer

What We Do

- Not fearful, but trust the worthiness of God
- We are confident
- We pray, we seek, we ask
- We meditate in His temple
- We wait upon the Lord
- We seek the Lord's face
- We desire to be in the house of the Lord
- We sing praises with joy
- We ask of God our petitions (prayer)
- We take courage

What a wonderful section of Scripture that lets us be exposed to God's character and how we as a couple might respond to Him! Being a Christian involves more than merely going to church and saying a few token prayers. As David shares today, God responds to us and we must respond to Him. Discuss with your mate how wonderful God is.

Prayer

Father God, it's hard to realize what a magnificent being You are. We try the best we can, but our minds aren't big enough. As we read Your Word we thank men like David, who took the time many centuries ago to write down his conversations with You. Thank You, also, for selecting David to be Your messenger. We appreciate all the truths we have learned from today's reading. Instill in us a desire to search Your Word and chew on it until we are able to swallow it into our very being. Amen.

Taking Action

- Select one truth from each of the four sections and meditate upon their truths.
- What does each mean?
- How can I respond to this truth?
- Select at least one response and act it out today in your life.

Reading On

Psalm 25:12
Psalm 37:4

Five Qualities of Healthy Couples

1. Healthy couples have a clearly defined menu of expectations. When a family agrees on a menu of options for quality life and relationships, they'll enjoy a healthy, successful family.

2. Healthy couples understand and practice meaningful communication. Within marital and family communication, it's important to remember that you're trying to move toward the deepest level of intimacy.

3. Healthy couples are associated with a small, healthy support group. Meet regularly with three or four other couples who have the same commitment to God and their marriages that you have.

4. Healthy couples are aware of unhealthy or offensive behavior stemming from their heritage. The Bible says that the sins of a father are visited on the children up to four generations. I must realize that what I'm doing to my wife and children today could be directly related to my great grandfather.

5. Healthy couples have a vibrant relationship with Jesus Christ. When Jesus permeates our relationship as a family we experience a calm and quiet spirit—we also know that He is our source of life.

—*Gary Smalley*
in *Seven Promises of a Promise Keeper*

Six People Stand at the Altar

Scripture Reading: Psalm 139:1-24

Key Verse: Psalm 139:23

> *Search me, O God, and know my heart; test me and know my anxious thoughts.*

---————— ☙ ——————---

A mature pastor friend of ours shares that when he is doing premarital counseling with a couple there are actually six people who stand before him at the wedding ceremony:

The Groom
- The man he thinks he is
- The man you think he is
- The man he really is

The Bride
- The woman she thinks she is
- The woman you think she is
- The woman she really is

One of the secrets of a successful marriage is for each partner to realize and live out who he or she really is.

Only when we stand before God in absolute truth can we as mates move in the direction that God has for us.

Remember that God is the One who knows all about our beginning and our ending. He knows our genealogy and He made every cell in our body. He is familiar with our emotions and any physical disability. He is waiting for us to acknowledge that He knows everything about us.

One of our sins is to hide from others our true selves. We are afraid that people would not like or love us if they only knew what we are really like. So we spend much of our life hiding from ourselves. Only until we can humbly go to God and extend our arms and hands up toward heaven and shout, "Search me, O God, and know my heart; test me and know my anxious thoughts!" can we ever begin to know our true selves.

As a couple, one of our goals is to become one (Genesis 2:24,25) and to be able to stand before God naked and not be ashamed. This doesn't mean just physical nakedness but all of our guilts, anxieties, and past sins of omission and commission.

Today may you and your spouse do away with the first four people at the marriage altar and concentrate upon becoming that third and sixth person: the real man and woman.

What a freeing spirit to become true on the outside as well as the inside! Stop your hiding today and stand before your mate naked and unashamed.

Prayer

Father God, what a relief to know that I can know myself as You know me! My prayer for today is that both of us will become true to ourselves. We

no longer want to hide behind the facade of false-
hoods. Take these negative energies and apply them
positively to honor and worship You, Your Son, and
Your Spirit. Amen.

Taking Action

- Risk possible failure by sharing with your spouse
  one lie of pretense that you want to change today.

- Ask your mate to pray for this decision and to
  hold you accountable to this decision.

- Note in your journal what you have decided to do
  today.

Reading On

Genesis 2:24,25
Romans 8:18-27

Learn to fill your days up, one at a time. Don't try to fill the void all at once. Find your loneliest day; fill it half up with fun and friends. Then concentrate on one other day. Once you have done this with several days in your week, you'll find that the quality of your life has improved, and much of your depression will have turned to joy and much more of your anxiety—your cover-up loneliness—will have gone.

—*Toby Rice Drews*

Drudgery Is No Fun

Scripture Reading: 2 Corinthians 6:3-11

Key Verse: 2 Corinthians 6:4

> . . . in great endurance, in troubles, hardships and distresses.

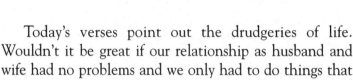

Today's verses point out the drudgeries of life. Wouldn't it be great if our relationship as husband and wife had no problems and we only had to do things that were a lot of fun? Our society says, "Only do it if it feels good." Yet if we did only the feel-good things in life we would never have the opportunity to experience those things that develop true Christian character.

If we rise up and let our lives shine during the doing of drudgery tasks we can witness transfiguration that makes drudgery divine.

How do we transform the mundane into the divine? The Scripture for today says that as servants of God we commend ourselves in every way in:

- great endurance
- troubles
- hardships
- hunger
- purity
- understanding

- distresses
- beatings
- imprisonments
- riots
- hard work
- sleepless nights

- patience
- kindness
- in the Holy Spirit
- in sincere love
- in truthful speech
- in the power of God

with weapons of righteousness in the right hand and in the left, through glory and dishonor, bad report and good report . . . beaten and yet not killed; sorrowful, yet always rejoicing; poor, yet making many rich; having nothing and yet possessing everything.

Yes, Paul knew how to take the drudgeries of life and turn them into something divine.

How can we today take all of our drudgeries—

- work
- children
- marriage
- loss of job
- loss of health
- not enough money

- laundry
- yardwork
- repair the broken appliances
- fix the car
- clean the garage

and make them divine? Only when we become servants to each other and let the Holy Spirit strengthen us beyond our human efforts.

Oswald Chambers says, "Drudgery is one of the finest touchstones of character there is. Drudgery is work that is very far removed from anything to do with the ideal—the utterly mean, grubbing things; and when we come in contact with them we know instantly whether or not we are spiritually real."[9]

Drudgery must have the inspiration of God in order for us to see it in His proper light. Christ's death on the cross was certainly the greatest form of drudgery, but it was vitally necessary for our salvation.

As a couple, none of our drudgeries will ever be that demanding.

Prayer

> *Father God, as we look upon the everyday drudgeries of our life may we recognize our servanthood to You. May we see eternal light in these tasks, so that we can recognize that You are building eternal character in our lives. May we as Mom and Dad also pass along these principles of life to our children so they too will recognize the virtues of things that are not always a lot of fun.*

Taking Action

- Examine two or three of your drudgeries to see how God can make these into virtues.

- Identify one of these drudgeries today and say, "I am going to conquer the negative voice that is inside me that's telling me—this is no fun." Take Satan's negative and turn it into a godly positive.

Reading On

John 13:1-17
Hebrews 13:5

This Big Mess Is a Blessing

Scripture Reading: 1 Timothy 5:1-15

Key Verse: 1 Timothy 5:8

> *If anyone does not provide for his relatives, and especially for his immediate family, he has denied the faith and is worse than an unbeliever.*

———— ✆ ————

"Billy, would you please help with the dishes tonight? I've had such a hard day at work and I just don't have the energy to do one more thing." Billy's reply is like that of many teenagers, "But Mom, I wasn't the only one to make the mess. The rest of the family needs to help out too. I just hate dirty dishes. Why can't we use paper plates?"

Does this conversation sound familiar to you? Who likes the mess that goes with a meal? Wouldn't it be great if somehow the dishes took care of themselves? But of course they don't; messes do need attention.

Much of life is how we look at things. Are we positive or are we negative? Is our glass half-full or half-empty?

Let's see if we can turn the messes of our life into blessings. In order for us to have dirty dishes, it means that we have eaten food, and in most cases more food than we need. We have leftovers, which means we have an abundance of food. Let's thank God for the abundance of food rather than the mess it makes. In America most of us are truly blessed to have enough food on our table.

Let's teach our family members to thank God for giving us enough food so we can have dirty dishes from that food. How many of our other messes are simply evidence that God has given us abundance? Let's look at our messes in a new light: How are they signs of abundance?

- How about clothes that need washing and ironing?
- Lawns that need to be mowed?
- Beds that need to be made?
- Carpets that need vacuuming?
- A refrigerator that needs cleaning?
- A school that we need to walk to?
- A job that we need to drive to?
- A home that needs painting?
- A television that needs repairs?

Prayer

Father God, thank You for showing me that I need to be reminded that our messes are really a sign of abundance and that You are the One who so richly gives to us, Your children. We do thank You for all that You give our family. Thank You for our home, our food, our clothes, our appliances, our schools, and our jobs. I truly want to look at our abundance and not our messes. Amen.

Taking Action

- As a family discuss the messes of your lives.
- How are they really indications that God has given us abundance?

- Thank God for all your messes that have become blessings.
- Make it a habit to give God a prayer of thanks before each meal.

Reading On

Ephesians 4:25-28
Luke 12:15

Remain Loyal to God

Scripture Reading: Romans 8:28-31

Key Verse: Romans 8:28

> *We know that in all things God works for the good of those who love him, who have been called according to his purpose.*

———— ✍ ————

This promise is reserved for the children of God. Sometimes this promise is given to an unbeliever in order to give him or her comfort during the death of a loved one, a bad failure in business, or even a failed marriage. When we use this verse improperly it may give comfort, but this promise is only for the believer who has been chosen by God to be one of His children.

This verse is also a test of our loyalty to God. Are we only fair-weather Christians? Or can we remain loyal to God even during the difficult times of our lives? Can we still see God's purpose for us in times of illness, death, lack of food, lack of work, lack of money, lack of home, and lack of family?

In our culture today we are challenged to remain loyal to our work, to our sports team, to our country, to our school, and to our marriage, but seldom are we encouraged to remain loyal to God through all situations.

Larry Crabb reminds his readers in *The Marriage Builder* that the hope of the Christian lies not in a change of circumstances, which God may or may not bring about, but in the grace of God. We aren't to hope that the circumstances will change, but we are to hope in God's grace—in His unearned, undeserved, and unconditional love for us.

God promises to permit only those events to enter our lives that will further His purpose in our lives. Our responsibility is to respond to life's events in a way that will please the Lord, and not to try to change the circumstances into what we want.[10]

The idea is not that we work for God, but because of our loyalty to Him He can work through us.

Remember that God is the Potter and we are the clay. He wants to conform us to His own image, not our image. In the '90s culture this fact is hard to live out, since we live in a "now" environment. We only want to do things that feel good right now. Many of life's character-building circumstances don't feel good—in fact, they hurt and are quite painful. They are events that we wouldn't choose for ourselves.

As a couple reaffirm your loyalty to God today. Acknowledge that He is God and that He only permits those events to come into our lives that are life-forming for us.

Prayer

> *Father God, as we come to You today we want to be loyal to You, but humanly speaking we are fearful that You won't look after us as well as we will look after ourselves. Only by the Scriptures*

and the grace that You give us can we enter into this trust. However, today we reconfirm our trust and loyalty to You. Use us in whatever way You can be glorified. We are empty vessels to be filled by Your purposes. We want to be used. Amen.

Taking Action

- Give your mate, your family, your job, and your possessions to the Lord.
- Acknowledge that everything you have is on loan from God; He is the Potter and you are the clay.

Reading On

Romans 11:29
1 Corinthians 1:9

A New Kind of Commitment

All of my life I had been influenced too much by the moods of my associates. When they were excited and panicked, I reflected their anxiety. Now . . . although I was still performing in the same circles . . . I was occasionally finding a calmness and an ability to love with more honesty and integrity than before. I was starting to play my life to a different audience—to the Living Christ . . . . I began to get up in the morning being conscious of God's awareness of me and my waking movements. I began being able to tell Him that He was the One for whom I wanted to perform the day's actions. Just the conscious act of deciding that was a new kind of commitment which, by itself, changed all kinds of things.

—*Keith Miller*

In Humility
Consider Others

Scripture Reading: Philippians 2:1-8

Key Verse: Philippians 2:5

> *Your attitude should be the same as that of Christ Jesus.*

———— ⊛ ————

Have you heard of the pastor who was given a badge for being the most humble person in the church? The badge was taken back when he wore it!

Humility. It's hard to get a handle on. What exactly is it?

I stood in the upstairs hallway, looking down over the banister and waiting for the younger children to come in for their baths. My oldest daughter, taking a piano lesson, was in the living room directly below, and the repetitive melody she was playing echoed through my mind.

I noticed, however, that one of my young sons was trudging slowly up the stairs, his bowed, grubby hands covering his small, dirt-streaked face. When he reached the top, I asked him what was wrong.

"Aw, nothing," he replied.

"Then why are you holding your face in your hands?" I persisted.

"Oh, I was just praying."

Quite curious now, I asked what he was praying about.

"I can't tell you," he insisted, "because if I do, you'll be mad."

After much persuasion I convinced him that he could confide in me and that, whatever he told me, I would not get mad. So he explained that he was praying about a problem he had with his mind.

"A problem with your mind?" I asked, now more curious than ever, wondering what kind of problem a child of six could have with his mind. "What kind of problem?"

"Well," he said, "You see, every time I pass by the living room, I see my piano teacher, and my tongue sticks out."

Needless to say, it was hard to keep a straight face, but I took his problem seriously and assured him that God could indeed help him with it.

Later, on my knees beside the bathtub as I bathed this little fellow, I thought how I still struggle with the problem of controlling my mind and my tongue. That afternoon as I knelt to scrub that sturdy little body, the tub became my altar; the bathroom, my temple. I bowed my head, covered my face, and acknowledged that I, like my son, had a problem with my mind and tongue. I asked the Lord to forgive me and to give me more and more the mind and heart and attitude of Christ."[11]

With the media constantly bombarding us with messages about self-esteem, it's easy to be confused about what genuine humility is. Having the mind and heart and attitude of Christ is a good start, and verse three of today's passage adds this: "Do nothing out of selfish ambition or vain conceit, but in humility consider others better than yourselves."

As we study the life of Christ, we see that His willingness to serve had its roots in His confidence that God loved Him. Jesus found strength and security in knowing how valuable He was to His Father. This knowledge of His Father's love enabled Jesus to serve people and ultimately die for us sinful human beings. Likewise, knowing our value to God through Christ is our first step toward true humility.

It is out of strength, not weakness, that we grow in humility. Bruce Narramore states that humility has three elements:

- Recognize that you need God;
- A realistic evaluation of your abilities;
- A willingness to serve.[12]

Are those three elements in place in your life? They are aspects of true humility and are vitally necessary if we are to serve in God's kingdom.

Prayer

> *Father God, You know how self-centered I am. You know how I'm always busy with something and how I hate to be inconvenienced. I need to learn to give myself away to others. Teach me humility. Teach me to serve as Christ did. Amen.*

Taking Action

- Do you recognize your need for God? If so, thank God for that awareness. If not, why not?

- Evaluate your abilities. List six strengths and six weaknesses. What are you going to do for the kingdom of God with your strengths? What plans do you have for turning your weaknesses into strengths?

- In what three capacities or organizations would you be willing to serve? Step forward and volunteer your services in one of these areas this week.

Reading On

Philippians 2:8,9   James 1:26-3:18
Psalm 39:1-13

Do all the good you can, by all the means you can, in all the ways you can, in all the places you can, to all the people you can, as long as ever you can.

—*John Wesley*

Is God's Joy in You?

Scripture Reading: John 15:1-17

Key Verse: John 15:11

> *I have told you this so that my joy may be in you and that your joy may be complete.*

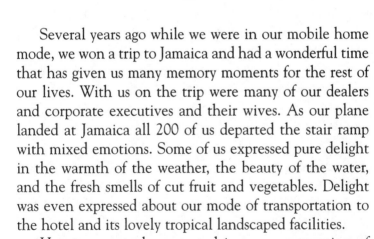

Several years ago while we were in our mobile home mode, we won a trip to Jamaica and had a wonderful time that has given us many memory moments for the rest of our lives. With us on the trip were many of our dealers and corporate executives and their wives. As our plane landed at Jamaica all 200 of us departed the stair ramp with mixed emotions. Some of us expressed pure delight in the warmth of the weather, the beauty of the water, and the fresh smells of cut fruit and vegetables. Delight was even expressed about our mode of transportation to the hotel and its lovely tropical landscaped facilities.

However, as to be expected in any cross-section of people, some expressed their disdain for all the same features that most of us were joyful about. Our mouths hung open in disbelief at the many disgruntled vacationers in such a romantic and gorgeous setting topped off by the most ideal climate you would ever want to experience.

The next morning as we approached the elevators to take us to the main lobby for breakfast, we were met by the most delightful group of young native Jamaican housekeepers. They were singing, laughing, and thanking God for such a beautiful new day. All of a sudden we were made aware of the contrast between the various groups at their hotel. Many of the wealthiest members of our group were moaning in negative tones, yet these low-income young ladies (probably working for less than our minimum wage in the States) were expressing sheer joy for their abundance! Later we were to find out that these housekeepers went to mission schools and had been grounded in the fundamentals of the Christian faith.

In our passage today Jesus is teaching about the vine and its branches and how it relates to producing good or bad fruit. He tells the reader that He (Jesus) has told this so that Jesus' joy may be in you and that your joy may be complete.

These young girls certainly reflected the joy of Jesus in their behavior and their testimony to the people around them. They weren't joyful because of status, wealth, or possessions, but because Jesus told them they could have His joy. It's that simple: Each day we can choose to be full of joy. We can respond to other people any way we want, but Scripture says that we can have the joy of Christ in our lives, and that it can be complete. This means it doesn't take any more than Jesus (no wealth, no status, no possessions), but just Jesus to make our joy complete. No longer can we say that we would have joy if only we had _____.

When teaching third-grade Sunday school I can remember writing on the chalkboard:

Jesus
O
You

I told these young children that joy meant that there was nothing between Jesus and you. And that's the gospel truth. In order to have joy, all we need is Jesus and ourselves —nothing more and nothing less.

Several other key Scriptures to challenge you as a couple in this joy area are:

- My meditation of the Lord will be sweet. I will be joyful in Him (from Psalm 104:34).
- Rejoice because your names are written in heaven (from Luke 10:20).
- You have shown me the paths that lead to life and Your presence will fill me with joy (from Acts 2:28).

Prayer

Father God, we truly want to reflect in our lives the joy that You have given us. There is a hurting world that is looking upon us to show them that there are rich blessings to being Your child. Let us as a couple decide that each day will be full of joy. Thank You for your radiance; life would be just a gloomy day without Your influence upon our lives. Amen.

Taking Action

- Commit to each other that you are going to reflect joy today by:_____, _____, and _____ (you insert the action).

- Ask this question around the table today and let each person contribute to the answer: "How do people show that they have joy in their lives?"

- Go around the table and share to the person on your left what he or she does to express joy to others.

- How can you share more joy in your life?

Reading On

Psalm 100:1   Luke 24:52,53
1 Samuel 2:1   John 17:13

The Joy of the Lord

God allows us to have disappointments, frustrations, or even worse because He wants us to see that our joy is not in such worldly pleasures as success or money or popularity or health or sex or even in a miracle-working faith; our joy is in the fact that we have a relationship with God. Few of us ever understand that message until circumstances have divested us of any possibility of help except by God Himself.

—Catherine Marshall

Knowing God's Will

Scripture Reading: Matthew 7:7-14

Key Verses: Matthew 7:13,14

> *Enter through the narrow gate. For wide is the gate and broad is the road that leads to destruction, and many enter through it. But small is the gate and narrow the road that leads to life, and only a few find it.*

We have often talked to mature Christians who say, "We want to do this, but we want to make sure we are in God's will." You might ask, "What is this thing called God's will? How do I know if I have it or not?"

There are two ways of living:

- We live for ourselves.
- We live for God.

When we live for ourselves we ignore God's will and follow our own desires. But when we seek to follow God's will, we want to obey Him and follow His path.

God has a will or a plan for each one of us. This is important for us to understand because He loves us. He knows what is best for us, even beyond our own expectations for ourselves. God doesn't want us to miss His plans for our lives. However, when we follow our own desires and ignore His will, we are not following what is best for our lives and we end up hurting ourselves, and sometimes the loved ones around us as well.

It may seem easier to ignore God's will, but it is a false path—a lie that Satan would like us to believe. In our Scripture today we have a warning to enter the narrow gate and not the broad one. The broad gate leads to destruction (the "everyone's doing it" mind-set). But small is the gate and narrow the road that leads to life, and only a few people find it.

One of our bumper stickers reads: "Successful people do what unsuccessful people aren't willing to do." Yes, to be successful in all branches of life we must be selective, focused, and disciplined; we must have a plan. Successful people always have a plan for life. Do you and your spouse have a plan? If not, today would be a good day to begin thinking about God's plan for your life.

How do we know God's will? We know it first of all through the pages of His Word, the Bible. This is one reason why it is important to make the Word of God part of our lives every day. In the Bible we find God's principles and directions for life. A few verses to help you reinforce this basic truth of His riches in Scripture are:

- I am not ashamed of the gospel because it is the power of God for salvation of everyone who believes (Romans 1:16).

- Blessed is the one who reads the words of the prophecy, and blessed are those who hear it and take to heart what is written in it, because the time is near (Revelation 1:3).

- The unfolding of your words gives light; it gives understanding to the simple (Psalm 119:130).

- These commands are a lamp, this teaching is a light, and the corrections of discipline are the way to life (Proverbs 6:23).

What to Pray For

I asked for bread and got a stone;
I used the stone to grind the grain
That made the flour to form the bread
That I could not obtain.
Instead of asking Him to give
The things for which we pray,
All that we need to ask
From God is this: Show us the way.

—James A. Bowman

In our lives we have found that it isn't as hard to *know* God's will as to *do* God's will. The knowledge seems easier than the action. By reading God's letters to us and by asking Him to show us His way, we can see that God wants only the best for our lives. Then we need to move out on faith in that direction. If we meet a detour along the way, we just detour and then keep on moving in the right direction. God's will is not always a straight line; sometimes there are curves in the way. Just keep on moving.

Prayer

Father God, help us to have a discerning spirit when it comes to knowing Your plan for our lives. Sometimes it seems such a mystery to us, but by faith we will study Your Word daily to receive your instructions for our time here on earth. Our prayers will bring us into contact with You and Your Holy Spirit. Thank You for being so concerned for us that You have a perfect plan just for us. Amen.

Taking Action

- In your journals write down two or three decisions that need to be made in your life.
- What would God's will be for each decision?
- Write down two or three activities for each decision that would put you into motion. Do step one today.

Reading On

Matthew 6:33   Romans 10:17
Philippians 4:13   Deuteronomy 11:18
Joshua 1:8

Do we carry about with us a sense of God? Do we carry the thought of Him with us wherever we go? If not, we have missed the greatest part of life. Do we have the feeling and conviction of God's abiding presence wherever we go?

—*Henry Drummond*

Love is Caring

Scripture Reading: James 1:19-26
Key Verses: James 1:22-24

> Do not merely listen to the word, and so deceive yourselves. Do what it says. Anyone who listens to the word but does not do what it says is like a man who looks to his face in a mirror and, after looking at himself, goes away and immediately forgets what he looks like.

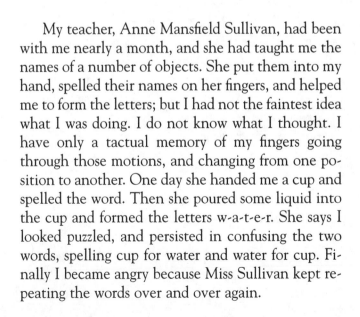

My teacher, Anne Mansfield Sullivan, had been with me nearly a month, and she had taught me the names of a number of objects. She put them into my hand, spelled their names on her fingers, and helped me to form the letters; but I had not the faintest idea what I was doing. I do not know what I thought. I have only a tactual memory of my fingers going through those motions, and changing from one position to another. One day she handed me a cup and spelled the word. Then she poured some liquid into the cup and formed the letters w-a-t-e-r. She says I looked puzzled, and persisted in confusing the two words, spelling cup for water and water for cup. Finally I became angry because Miss Sullivan kept repeating the words over and over again.

In despair she led me out to the ivy-covered pump house and made me hold the cup under the spout while she pumped. With her other hand she spelled w-a-t-e-r emphatically. I stood still, my whole body's attention fixed on the motions of her fingers as the cool stream flowed over my hand. All at once there was a strange stir within me—a misty consciousness, a sense of something remembered. It was as if I had come back to life after being dead. I understood that what my teacher was doing with her fingers meant the cold something that was rushing over my hand, and that it was possible for me to communicate with other people by these signs. It was a wonderful day never to be forgotten! . . . I think it was an experience somewhat in the nature of a revelation. . . . I wanted to learn the name of every object I touched, and before night I had mastered 30 words. . . . That first revelation was worth all those years I had spent in dark, soundless imprisonment. That word "water" dropped into my mind like the sun in a frozen winter world. Before that supreme event there was nothing in me except the instinct to eat and drink and sleep. My days were a blank without past, present, or future, without hope or anticipation, without interest or joy.[13]

—Helen Keller

So often we become inspired and brought to a higher plane of life only to turn our backs on the event and do nothing about it. We leave stating, "I'm going to _____," but we soon forget what we are going to do.

The love exhibited by the teacher Anne Mansfield Sullivan to her pupil Helen Keller is a remarkable example of a person who had an idea, wanted to care, and followed through with that idea by giving her adult life to teach a seemingly ordinary young girl named Helen. We are not all called to be that dedicated to one person, but many of us have been called to step out from the ordinary path of life to impact someone and his or her eternity.

As we review history we are brought face-to-face with great men and women who have affected the events of history. What did they possess? They each had a vision, and, once challenged, they followed through with the call. They didn't just say "I love you" then fall away from that passion. They all went the extra mile to really care.

At sometime in each of our lives we have been challenged to do something great—maybe at a retreat, by a powerful sermon by your pastor, by a television program, by a Sunday school teacher, by a teacher in school, or by a coach. This impact has made a real difference in your life, but maybe you've never gone beyond the commitment or thought stage. Now is the time to act it out.

In today's passage James tells us not to merely listen to the Word but to do what it says. This is true not only when reading Scripture but also when the Holy Spirit reveals truth in your heart. Several verses of Scripture can help you put your desires into action:

- Never be lacking in zeal, but keep your spiritual fervor, serving the Lord (Romans 12:11).
- He who works his land will have abundant food, but the one who chases fantasies will have his fill of poverty (Proverbs 28:19).
- The sluggard craves and gets nothing, but the

desires of the diligent are fully satisfied (Proverbs
13:4).

Be challenged today to work out your love by caring
for those around you. Don't be known as just a hearer of
the Word, but be a doer. It takes effort and sacrifice, and
not always doing what you want to do. It costs time and
money, and sometimes being disappointed by expecting
too much.

But wouldn't it be wonderful if all of your caring
would produce another Helen Keller!

Prayer

> *Father God, You know that we really want to
> be loving and caring people. We really want to fol-
> low through with all those good desires we have in
> life. Give us all the tools we need to truly love with
> care. Place upon our minds and hearts the one area
> of our desires which will result in the best fruit. Let
> us be diligent in our efforts to carry out the chal-
> lenges with ACTION. Amen.*

Taking Action

- As a couple, place in your journal three desires
  that you have to serve others.

- Discuss how you could implement these goals.

- What action will be necessary to get started?

  Money?

  Resources?

  Other people?

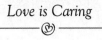
- What will be your first step? Be willing to get started now.

Reading On

1 Corinthians 13:1-13	Romans 12:3-8
Ephesians 4:1-16	Proverbs 24:30-34

Choose Love

Saying "Yes!" to God is not a simple matter because making our lives into lives of love is not a simple or easy thing. To choose love as a life principle means that my basic mind-set or question must be: What is the loving thing to be, to do, to say? My consistent response to each of life's events, to each person who enters and touches my life, to each demand on my time and nerves and heart, must somehow be transformed into an act of love. However, in the last analysis, it is this "Yes!" that opens me to God. Choosing love as a life principle widens the chalice of my soul, so that God can pour into me His gifts and graces and powers.

—*John Powell*

Healthy Christians
Share Their Faith

Scripture Reading: Luke 5:27-32
Key Verses: Luke 5:31,32

> *It is not the healthy who need a doctor, but the sick. I have not come to call the righteous, but sinners to repentance.*

───────── ☙ ─────────

This story of Jesus sharing the good news to despised tax collectors was disturbing to the religious leaders of His day, but it certainly pointed out that His priority was to be out and among sinners.

In order for us to share our faith with others, our faith must first have an object, and that object is the Person of Jesus Christ. Often we say we don't have the time, the gift, or the personality to share the gospel. One of our favorite verses in this regard is 2 Timothy 1:7,8: "God did not give us a spirit of timidity, but a spirit of power, of love and of self discipline. So do not be ashamed to testify about our Lord."

As we exercise this part of our faith, we are to ask God for a spirit of power and love for those who are drifting along in life with no purpose or cause.

When we begin to share the gospel, we can share

what Christ has done for us. We can tell people that He has changed us from a sinner to a forgiven sinner, and that He has rearranged the priorities in our life. We have had a heart transplant, and we became a new creature in Christ. What used to make us a prisoner has set us free to be all that God wants us to be. If we can talk to our friends about sports, politics, movies, weather, vacations, and favorite restaurants, then we can certainly share what Jesus has done for us!

Our Scripture today also reminds us that sharing our faith means that we have to put up with opposition from both the Christian and non-Christian community. The religious leaders of the day asked His disciples why Jesus ate and drank with tax collectors and sinners. You too will find those who want to set you straight on your methodology or content of sharing. With so much bad going on in this world there will be well-meaning people who attack your goodness. Often people would rather remain in darkness than be exposed by the light of the good news.

When we share our faith we will sometimes run into people who have never heard of this Person called Jesus. We will discover that many around us are lost, and that if they were to die in their present state they would be judged to eternal life separated from God. In 1 John 5:13 the writer tells us why he has written all the words about Jesus: "I write these things to you who believe in the name of the Son of God so that you may know that you have eternal life."

We share our faith so that people will hear about the Son of God and find eternal life. The message and purpose have been the same for almost 2000 years.

A healthy Christian is one who shares his faith. Exactly how you do it depends upon your style and abilities. As Jesus answered the religious leaders of His day, "It is not the healthy who need a doctor, but the sick. I have not come to call the righteous, but sinners to repentance." Reach out to those who are lost. Get out of your comfort zone and be challenged by new faces and new places.

Prayer

> *Father God, please show us as a couple how we can share our faith to those around us. We feel so timid at times. Give us the power of the Holy Spirit and Your eternal love for those who are lost. We realize that there will be those who don't understand us and what we are doing, but give them a spirit of encouragement and not the seeds for criticism. Please make available to us those who have teachable spirits. Amen.*

Taking Action

- Write in your journals the names of three to five individuals or couples with whom you would like to share the good news.

- Consider inviting each of these people into your homes within the next six months to have dinner with you.

- If opportunity presents itself, share what being a Christian has meant to you and how it has changed your life.

- Share Christ through lifestyle evangelism. Let people see you in real-life situations. Let them see you as an everyday real person who has the same problems that they have but who has found the answers to life through Jesus Christ.

Reading On

Acts 13:38   1 John 3:5
1 John 2:1,2   1 Timothy 1:15

Giving with a Faith Promise

Scripture Reading: Deuteronomy 8:1-20

Key Verses: Deuteronomy 8:17,18

> *You may say to yourself, "My power and the strength of my hands have produced this wealth from me." But remember the Lord your God, for it is he who gives you the ability to produce wealth.*

———⊗———

A Christian boy once decided to give a tenth of his money to God. But when he won a money prize for an essay on a religious topic, he felt he could not give less than a fifth of the award to the church. Ever since then he was not able to deny himself the pleasure of giving a fifth.

God wonderfully blessed this young man, and increased his financial means and his enjoyment of doing good with his money. Legend has it that this young man became the great preacher C.H. Spurgeon.

Have you experienced the joy of giving to God? The Scriptures are full of teachings which pertain to money and giving:

- No one can serve two masters (Matthew 6:24).

- When you want to build a tower you sit down and calculate the cost (Luke 14:28-30).
- A faithful man will abound with blessings (Proverbs 28:20).
- Owe nothing to anyone (Romans 13:8).
- Where your treasure is, there will your heart be also (Matthew 6:21).
- The rich rules over the poor, and the borrower is servant to the lender (Proverbs 22:7).

I shall never forget how God taught me to give. I had been pastor of a large church in the city of Toronto. One day I resigned and on the first Sunday of January became pastor of a church which knew how to give in a way I had never known. I started in this pastorate at a time when the church was holding its annual missionary convention.

Now I knew nothing about a missionary convention. I didn't know the first thing to do. So I just sat on the platform and watched.

The ushers went down the aisles giving out envelopes. To my amazement, one had the audacity to hand me—the pastor!—an envelope. I can still remember that moment as though it were yesterday.

As I held the envelope I read, "In dependence upon God I will endeavor to give toward the missionary work of the church $_____ during the coming year." I did not know that God was going to deal with me that morning, and teach me a lesson that I was never to forget—a lesson that later I was to teach to hundreds of others.

I started to pray. I said, "Lord God, I can't do

anything. You know I have nothing. I haven't a cent in the bank. I haven't anything in my pocket. This church only pays me $25.00 a week. I have a wife and child. We are trying to buy our home; prices are sky high."

"I know that," the Lord seemed to answer me. "I know you are getting $25.00 a week. I know you have nothing in your pocket and nothing in the bank."

"Well, then," I said, relieved, "that settles it. I have nothing to give and I can't give anything." It was then the Lord spoke to my heart. I shall never forget it.

"I am not asking you for what you have," He said.

"You are not asking me for what I have, Lord?" I replied. "Then what are You asking?"

"I am asking you for a faith offering. How much can you trust Me for?"

"Oh, Lord," I exclaimed, "that's different. How much can I trust You for?"

Of course, I knew nothing about a faith offering. But I knew the Lord was speaking. I thought He might say $5.00 or perhaps even $10.00. I almost trembled as I awaited the answer. Then it came. Now of course God didn't speak to me in an audible voice, but He might just as well have.

"How much can I give?" I asked.

"Fifty dollars!" I exclaimed. "Why, Lord, that's two weeks' salary!"

But again the Lord spoke and it was still the same amount. It was just as clear to me as though He had spoken out loud.

My hand trembled as I signed my name and wrote in the amount—$50.00.

How I ever paid that amount I don't know to this day. All I know is that every month I had to pray for $4.00. And every month God provided it. At the end of the year I had paid $50.00. As I paid the final amount I realized I had received the greatest blessing of my life!

I had trusted God for a certain amount and He had met it. So great was the spiritual blessing that the next year at the convention, I doubled the amount and gave $100.00. Then at another convention I doubled the amount again and gave $200.00. At still another convention I doubled it once more and gave $400.00. Then later I doubled it again and made it $800.00. From that day to this I have been increasing the amount and sending it to the Bank of Heaven year by year. If I had waited until I had it, I never would have given it because I never would have received it. I gave a faith offering and God honored it.

That was the first time, I say, that I had ever given what I call a faith offering. The Apostle Paul often took up "faith promise offerings." He asked a church to promise a certain amount, and gave them a year to pay it. As the year drew to a close, he sent someone to remind the church of their faith promise before he arrived (see 2 Corinthians 9). A faith promise offering is a scriptural offering, it is a Pauline offering, and God blesses it.

Have you only given cash offerings? It requires little faith to give a cash offering. If I have a dollar in my pocket, all I have to do is take it out and put it on the plate. I don't have to ask God for it. I don't have to trust Him for any definite amount. I just have it and give it.

But it is entirely different with a faith promise offering. I have to pray and ask God how much He would have me give, then trust Him for it. Month by month I must go to Him in prayer and ask Him for the amount promised. I must wait upon Him until it comes in. What a blessing such dependence brings!

For well over a quarter of a century now, that is the kind of offering I have taken for missions. In our annual missionary convention we never get more than six or seven thousand dollars in cash, but we get a quarter of a million or more in faith promises! And it always comes in! More comes in than the amount promised!

I am not talking about pledges. A pledge offering is between you and a church, between you and a missionary society. Some day the deacons may collect it, or you may receive a letter reminding you of it. You can be held responsible for a pledge offering.

A faith promise offering is between you and God. No official will ever call on you to collect it. No one will ever send you a letter about it. If you are unable to pay it, all you have to do is to tell God about it. Give Him your reason. If He accepts it, you are free.

This, my friend, is the greatest investment you can make. You should be in business for God. You should make money for Him, use what you need to live on and give as much as you can for the work of evangelization. Put your money where it will accomplish the most for God. Put it into the getting out of the Gospel. Put it into the souls of men. Use it for those who have never heard the message.

Perhaps God would have you support a missionary or Christian organization and then another, and another. Make a faith promise offering unto Him, then trust Him to help you meet it. Unmeasurable blessing will be yours.[14]

Prayer

Father God, thank You today for reminding us that we are in the ministry to evangelize the world through the spreading of the gospel. We thank You for giving us this pastor's experience with a faith promise. This certainly falls under grace and not under the law. May we as a couple branch out in our Christian walk and begin to experience in a greater way investing in Your work. Amen.

Taking Action

- As a couple discuss how you can begin implement giving by a faith promise to God's work.

- What areas of the budget will you need to look at? What cuts need to be made?

- As a couple and family make a commitment to give regularly to _____, _____, _____ organizations. If you need help identifying worthy organizations make an appointment with your pastor to review such opportunities.

Reading On

Proverbs 23:4,5   1 Timothy 6:17-19
Ecclesiastes 4:6   Proverbs 22:22

Don't turn away from any man saying that you have nothing to give or lend—you have. If you're Christ's you have something to contribute to that man's need.

—E. Stanley Jones

The Art of Good Teaching

Scripture Reading: Deuteronomy 6:1-9
Key Verses: Deuteronomy 6:6,7

> *These commandments that I give you today are to be upon your hearts. Impress them on your children. Talk about them when you sit at home and when you walk along the road, when you lie down and when you get up.*

————————ᗏ————————

Our goal as parents is to bring out the very best in our children. There are many techniques out there that tell you how to be good parents. Some are valuable and some will be short-lived because they don't have value behind them (your values). In order for techniques to work, they must be part of your belief system. Business and education constantly look into new areas of research to find out what makes good managers and teachers. The common strand for success in both of these areas is to have a genuine caring attitude for the people they are responsible for.

That is true of parenting too. To be effective, you must show your children that you really care for them—not just in words but also in action. They are continually

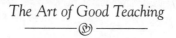
asking in their music, friends, clothes, and grades, "Do you really love me?"

As parents we want to know how to carry out this genuine caring. Here are 10 qualities that exhibit good parenting:

• *Really listen.* This means to turn off the radio or TV and put down the newspaper or magazine so that you can give 100 percent of your attention to your conversation. Tell the other members of the family that you are not to be disturbed unless for a major emergency. Be like one parent who said, "I hear not only with my ears, but with my eyes and my guts. I don't want to miss anything, either verbally or nonverbally."

• *Take an interest in your children as people.* Be interested in them as people, and not only as your children. Ask them questions: How did school go? How's Mary? How's football? How's church? How's your stomachache? Care about them.

• *Be clear in your expectations.* Tell your children what you expect and then give them freedom to do it. Each child may do things differently, based upon his or her temperament. Some children do things with little flair while others do things with great flair.

• *Be willing to transmit your knowledge to your children eagerly.* Take time to explain, demonstrate, and answer their questions even if they seem simple to you. Give them time when you're walking, when you lie down, and when you get up.

• *Reinforce positive behaviors and discourage unacceptable performance.* Compliment good work by making children know what specifically is being praised. This way you are more likely to get repeat performances. Conversely, by being specific about what needs to be improved, you teach children to perform at a higher level than they normally do.

• *Trust your children to fulfill their promises.* Train them how to keep their word. One of our favorite mottoes is, "Just do what you say you are going to do." We are to keep our word by keeping our appointments, calling back when we say we will, and turning in our homework assignments on time. Let your children work out the details by themselves.

• *Be flexible and remain open to good ideas.* Admit when you are wrong and be willing to change your mind when the evidence shows you are wrong. Don't think you have all the answers. Let answers to the questions come from all members of the family.

• *Have a good sense of humor.* Humor and enthusiasm are infectious and create a friendly, productive atmosphere. Learn to laugh at yourself. It's more fun to be in a family that can laugh with each other and not at each other.

• *Challenge and set standards that raise the standards.* Search for excellence, not perfection. Lift the members of the family to a notch higher than they would reach by themselves.

• *Stay in control of the family unit.* Even if things go astray, the family members will stay loyal and supportive of its leadership if the leaders are in control. That means in language, body motions, attitudes, temperament, and balance. We as parents must exhibit the highest standards for ourselves. We can't ask our children to go beyond a standard that we don't exhibit ourselves. Is your family a caring family?

Prayer

Father God, we realize that we are not always consistent in our caring attitude with members of our family. Thank You for giving us several areas that make for healthy families. We certainly want a family that reflects a caring attitude not only among the family unit, but also to those we know. Thank You for caring for us. We wouldn't be where we are today without Your caring for us. Amen.

Taking Action

- Identify with your mate the top three strengths that your family exhibits from today's ten areas.

- Identify the two or more areas that you need improvement in. What will you do to strengthen these areas?

- Take the risk of sharing these areas with your children. Solicit from them areas that could be improved.

- Write each of your children an uplifting note about him or her and place it under his pillow to be found and read tonight when he goes to bed.

Reading On

Isaiah 54:13 Mark 10:14-16
Psalm 127:3-5 Proverbs 17:6

What Makes a Home?

Scripture Reading: Psalm 127:1-5

Key Verse: Psalm 127:1

> Unless the Lord builds the house, its builders labor in vain.

As parents we sometimes wonder if we actually have a home, or is it merely a stopover place to eat, do laundry, hang around, and sleep? Is it just a place to repair, mow the lawn, pay off the mortgage, paint, wallpaper, install new carpet, and get quick cash? A true home is much more than all that; it is a place of people living, growing, dying, laughing, crying, learning, and creating together.

A small child was once quoted after watching his house burn down, "We still have a home. We just don't have a house to put it in." How perceptive!

Our home should be a trauma center for the whole family. We don't have to be perfect—just forgiven. We can grow, we can make mistakes, we can laugh, we can cry, we can agree, we can disagree. Home should be a place where happy experiences occur—a place sheltered from the problems of the world and a place of love, acceptance, and security. When we read the morning newspaper we are confronted with all the tragedies around us and we realize that the world outside our front door is falling apart, but within our four walls we can offer a place called home.

What can we do to have a home like God intended? As with everything in life, when something is broken we go back to the instruction book. In this case it is the Bible. The home is God's idea—not something invented by twentieth-century Americans. In the original plan of God's creation He designed the home to be the foundation of society, a place to meet the mental, spiritual, physical, and emotional needs of people.

Scripture states that the family is a permanent relationship not to be divided. Marriage is instituted by God to accomplish His plans in our society. In marriage a husband and wife become "one" (Genesis 2:24), building a permanent relationship. It is not a temporary convenience to be upheld as long as it's fun and feels good. God designed the family as a permanent relationship in which with His care humans could weather the storms of life together. The home is God's loving shelter for growing to maturity.

Even though God designed marriage, family, and home to be a permanent relationship, it isn't automatic. The members of the family must work together at making a true home. As parents we are responsible to lead the way. We are to direct the paths for our children, to show the way.

Loving and living with your partner and children takes determination and practice, plus time and imagination, sacrifice, planning, and a lot more. It takes more than just love and determination. In our key verse for today we read, "Unless the Lord builds the house, its builders labor in vain." God is not only the designer, but He also wants to occupy the headship of family life. He wants to guide and to give love, peace, and forgiveness abundantly.

Solomon spoke to this subject in Proverbs 24:3,4: "By wisdom a house is built, and through understanding it is established; through knowledge its rooms are filled with rare and beautiful treasures." Solomon's "big three" in home construction is:

- Wisdom
- Understanding
- Knowledge

We've got our work cut out for us if we want a true home. We can't do a very good job unless we roll up our sleeves and get busy. There's not much time to be listless and nondirected. We must live life with a big purpose—to have not just a house but a home.

In order to do this seemingly impossible task we must yield our heart, soul, and life to God's Son, Jesus Christ. The future of your family and your eternal destiny depends on your relationship with God. If you haven't accepted Jesus as your personal Savior (not as a couple but individually), do so today. Make Him the center of your life and home.

Read the Bible each day to gain guidance for your life and family. Pray that God will help you fulfill your family responsibility, realizing that He wants to help your family to be a testimony to the world. If you are not already doing so, seek out a Bible-believing church together. We all need the encouragement and fellowship of other Christians as well as instruction in God's Word.

With Christ as Lord of your family you can have a happy home. If you yield to Him daily your home can be more than just a "place"; it can be a true family—living, growing, and learning together with God.[15]

Prayer

> *Father God, You know we want our home to be more than just a place. We want it to be a home where You have the throne. We want to yield to Your leadership. Give us wisdom, understanding, and knowledge to see us through this seemingly impossible task of making a home. Thank You for giving us your Instruction Manual. May we read it each day to gain Your insight. We personally feel so inadequate, but with Your power we can do it. Thank You for Your help. Amen.*

Taking Action

- Settle the lordship of your home today. If you aren't a "child of God," become one now by trusting Jesus Christ.

- Pray for your home and its various members.

- What are you going to do to make your house a home? Ask your spouse to help you commit to these goals.

- Begin today.

Reading On

Romans 3:23	Romans 6:23
1 Peter 3:18	Ephesians 5:15—6:4

Today Is Special

Scripture Reading: Psalm 89:15-18

Key Verse: Psalm 89:15

> *Blessed are those who have learned to acclaim*
> *you, who walk in the light of your presence,*
> *O Lord.*

———————— ⊛ ————————

Today is not just an ordinary day. It's one like no other day we have ever lived. "This is the day the Lord has made; let us rejoice and be glad in it" (Psalm 118:24). No matter if it's raining, snowing, blowing, or boiling, we need to rejoice and be glad in this day. Let's do something special: Make a new meal or clothes item, stroll through the park, fly a kite with the children, paint the bathroom, clean out a closet.

Today is not an ordinary day. Today God has opened new opportunities, the past is history, and the future won't be until tomorrow. Today is all we can live. So let's celebrate. Let's read a poem, write a poem, write a song, or sing a song of praise. God delights in showering us with His very special blessings. "Every good and perfect gift is from above, coming down from the Father of the heavenly lights, who does not change like shifting shadows" (James 1:17).

Today is a special day because we realize that God freely offers us His best gifts to enjoy. In John 10:10 Jesus states, "I have come that they may have life, and have it to the full." He wants us to have a full and abundant life. He has spread a banquet for us.

Since this is a special day, let's thank God for this free gift of life. Let's praise Him for who He is. Let's trust Him for the days to come. This abundant life fills the God-void in our lives, and it also provides us with power to overcome the problems of life. So step out in faith and give Jesus all your cares!

Prayer

> *Father God, let us rejoice in this day that You have given to us. We want to count our blessings. Let us look at today as a gift from You. We want to be good stewards of Your time. No matter what comes into our lives today, we know You have screened it so that we are capable of handling it. We want to rejoice and be glad in this day. Amen.*

Taking Action

- Write in your journal five things that are a blessing to you.

- Do something special today. What might it be?

- Provide something special to a special person in your life: a card, a gift, a telephone call, a fax, etc.

- Tell each member of your family why he or she is special to you.

- Discuss around the evening table this question: "Why was today so special?"

Reading On

Isaiah 55:12	Psalm 126:5,6
Psalm 4:7	1 Peter 1:8

When we lose waking up in the morning as though each day was going to be full of adventure, joys, and dangers, and wake up instead to the alarm clock (as most of us must; and how lovely those rare nights when we look at the clock and don't have to set the alarm), and the daily grind, and mutter about TGIF, we lose the newborn quality of belief which is so lovely in the child.

—*Madeline L'Engle*

I Need to Forgive

Scripture Reading: Matthew 6:12-15

Key Verse: Matthew 6:12

> *Forgive us our debts, as we also have forgiven our debtors.*

———————⊗———————

In our hearts we sometimes store unforgiven words to God, to ourselves, to a family member, to a neighbor, or to someone at work. When we have not forgiven we become captive to that act and it holds us prisoner until we forgive. So we need to clean that slate of unforgiveness—to release and let go.

Forgiveness is very costly; there can be pain when we seek to forgive. Yet Jesus forgave while on the cross and we have to do it as well. True forgiveness from us to others isn't possible unless we have experienced God's forgiveness to us. We can't give away what we haven't experienced.

We first have to let God forgive us before we can forgive others. Out of our gratitude for God's forgiveness to us we are able to understand this whole area of forgiveness. When we are right with God we want to get right with others. The only person who is a slave to unforgiveness is ourself. When we consider this area of forgiveness we think of three groups of people:

- Those who need our forgiveness
- Those with whom we need to seek forgiveness
- Those who need our help in forgiving others.

Our longest list would probably be found in group two above. As in today's Scripture passage, Jesus says that we are to be forgiven of our sins as we forgive those who sin against us. We cannot be forgiven unless we forgive. Unconfessed forgiveness clogs up our spiritual arteries. We will never have good blood flow to our heart until we get rid of what clogs us up. God wants to go to our hearts, but we can't receive His blessings and abundance because we need to clean up this matter called forgiveness.

One of God's biblical principles is that unforgiving people cannot receive forgiveness. Jesus didn't say that it wouldn't be painful, for many times it is. However, to become fresh in our Christian walk we must clean the slate of all the marks we have logged against others. Then God can flow freely in our lives. First John 1:9 states, "If we confess our sins, he is faithful and just and will forgive us our sins and purify us from all unrighteousness."

On This Day

Mend a quarrel
Search out a forgotten friend
Dismiss a suspicion and replace it with trust
Write a letter to someone who misses you
Encourage a youth who has lost faith
Keep a promise
Forget an old grudge
Examine your demands on others and vow
to reduce them.

Fight for a principle
Express your gratitude
Overcome an old fear
Take two minutes to appreciate the beauty of nature
Tell someone you love them
Tell them again,
and again,
and again.[16]

—Frank R. Zelarney

Prayer

Father God, let us jump to forgive today. Today will be forgiveness day. We already know of several people with whom we are going to heal the rift that exists between us. When the sun goes down today we want to be healed from all that makes us ineffective Christians. Would You please go ahead of us and make the hearts before us tender and prepare them for our requests. We don't want to be dividers; we want to be healers and mediators with whom we live life. Thank You for the provisions of forgiveness. Amen.

Taking Action

- Reread the poem "On This Day."
- Choose two or three directions and apply them to your life today.
- Make today "Forgiveness Day."
- Make that first telephone call (or visit in person if possible).

Reading On

Matthew 5:44,45	Romans 12:20
Mark 11:25	Luke 6:35-38

Children Are a Heritage from the Lord

Scripture Reading: Psalm 127:1-5
Key Verses: Psalm 127:3-5

> *Sons are a heritage from the Lord, children a reward from him. Like arrows in the hands of a warrior are sons born in one's youth. Blessed is the man whose quiver is full of them. They will not be put to shame when they contend with their enemies in the gate.*

---— ☙ ——---

Entrepreneur and public speaker Wilson Harrell remembers his best teacher:

> When I was 11, my father made me a cotton buyer at his gin. Now I *knew* cotton, but I was well aware that my father was entrusting an 11-year-old with an awesome responsibility.
>
> When I cut a bale, I pulled out a wad, examined the sample, identified the grade and set the price. I'll never forget the first farmer I faced. He looked at me, called my father over and said, "Elias, I've worked too hard to have an 11-year-old boy decide what I'll live on next year."

My father was a man of few words. "His grade stands," he answered and walked away. Over the years my father never publicly changed my grade. However, when we were alone, he'd check my work. If I'd under-graded (and paid too little), I'd have to go tell the farmer I'd made a mistake and pay him the difference. If I'd overgraded, my fa-ther wouldn't say a word—he'd just look at me. It was worse than a world-class chewing out.

I'm not sure my father knew anything about entrepreneurship, but he understood an awful lot about making a man out of a boy. He gave me responsibility and then backed my hand. He also taught me that fairness builds a busi-ness and that the willingness to admit and cor-rect mistakes is a sure way to bring customers back.[17]

We as parents are encouraged to raise our children in the boundary of God's discipline and knowledge and ac-ceptance of His Son, Jesus. With that, Scripture says, they will have peace. As we look around at various children at school, in the malls, on vacation, or in the neighborhood, we find very few of them at peace. However, when we do find a child that reflects peace, we know where it comes from—a parent who knows the Lord and who has come to a very basic decision in his or her own life.

As parents we are to model the attributes of Christian character as listed in Galatians 5:22,23: "The fruit of the Spirit is:

Love
  Joy
    Peace
      Patience
        Kindness
          Goodness
            Faithfulness
              Gentleness
                Self-control."

Step out with a plan today to teach your children to be people with goodness to themselves and to others!

Prayer

> *Father God, You know that we want to teach our children according to Your principles. We don't want to move ahead of You. We want to give our children room to grow in their character development. Let us stand back when we want to overcorrect. May our children see us in the right perspective of our purest intent. Thank You, God, for these guiding principles. Amen.*

Taking Action

- What can you learn from today's lesson?

- How will you implement these ideas?

- Let one of your children decide what the evening meal will be, and have him or her help you in its preparation. Next week trade off with another child.

- Pop some popcorn for evening dessert.

Reading On

Acts 16:31	Acts 2:39
Isaiah 44:3	Psalm 128:3

We Belong in Families

No matter how difficult life becomes, we belong in families. There may be times when we let down those we love and fail people who care the most, but through it all we discover a group of people who make us feel that we belong, who say, "What happens to you matters to me." Thus we stand together and face all of life with a confidence born of a sure identity in the family. . . .

In spite of the pain, frustration and embarrassment, the unavoidable world of life in the family is still God's gift. The caring, nurture and confidence that comes from being seen at our worst and still knowing that we belong is His gift to us. It is the place where we can . . . love one another over the long haul. It is a place where we see His power and grace demonstrated over and over again.

—*John F. Westfall*

Happy Marriages Include

Scripture Reading: Philippians 4:4-9
Key Verse: Philippians 4:8

> *Finally, brothers, whatever is true, whatever is noble, whatever is right, whatever is pure, whatever is lovely, whatever is admirable—if anything is excellent or praiseworthy—think about such things.*

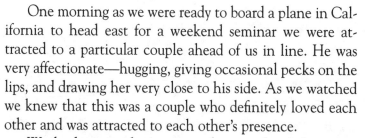

One morning as we were ready to board a plane in California to head east for a weekend seminar we were attracted to a particular couple ahead of us in line. He was very affectionate—hugging, giving occasional pecks on the lips, and drawing her very close to his side. As we watched we knew that this was a couple who definitely loved each other and was attracted to each other's presence.

We both wanted to get up close to this lady to see what she had going for her, because it was obvious that she had physical attractions to this young man. As they stood standing to the side, the rest of the line moved forward to board the plane. Were we surprised when we passed this couple still clinching each other! She wasn't like anything we envisioned, for we were startled to see a woman whose face had a lot of fresh scars from a recent severe automobile accident.

We passed somewhat in shock because here wasn't the physical beauty we expected to see, but we soon realized that we passed a man who went below the surface of this lady's physical presence and looked into her heart and soul, where he found eternal beauty.

Paul, the writer of today's verses, points out eight basic principles of thought and praise for finding happiness:

- Whatever is true
- Whatever is noble
- Whatever is right
- Whatever is pure
- Whatever is lovely
- Whatever is admirable
- If anything is excellent
- If anything is praiseworthy

THINK ABOUT SUCH THINGS.

Each morning as we begin a new day we have choices to make. One of these is to love our mate. We can choose to or choose not to—it is our choice. The happy individual and couple will make a decision each and every day to love their mate. Paul's eight guidelines for thought help us conquer all the negatives in the world.

As our mind drifts to the negatives of life we need to think on the above traits. Let's not get bogged down on the minors of life; let's stress the majors. With this biblical thought pattern we will begin to evaluate the food we eat, the movies we see, the literature we read, the music we hear, the friends we have, the TV programs we watch, and the words we speak. This Scripture will raise us to a higher standard of life. A scholar once stated, "Who we will be in the next five years will be based on three things: the books we read, the people we meet, and the choices we make." Today let us begin to think about such things.

Prayer

> *Father God, give us the willingness to think good thoughts today. Let us be uplifted and not downtrodden by our thoughts. Let me choose to love my mate so that others around us will know of our love for each other. Give us the ability to love unconditionally—beyond all external attractions. May this love overflow to others we meet. Amen.*

Taking Action

- Write down five things you like about your spouse.

- Write down on a slip of paper each night for a week three things you observed your mate doing for you. Exchange notes and discuss.

- Write down five things your mate had when you were dating that attracted him or her to you. Does he or she still have these same attractions? If not, why not? Discuss your answers between the two of you.

Reading On

Matthew 6:25-31   Ephesians 3:14-21
1 Corinthians 7:33,34   1 Peter 4:7-11

Love and Compatibility

Let's establish that love and compatibility are two very different things. Simply because we are profoundly attracted to people and have passionate feelings of love doesn't mean for a moment that we should *marry* them. Falling in love is easy. Some people can do it at the drop of a hat. But such people may have to fall in and out of love several times before they discover others with whom they could happily spend the rest of their lives.

There are also people with whom we are compatible, but whom we don't love. What we need is someone who is both.

We have been programmed by our culture, by the depiction of love on the screen, and by popular songs to think of love as the major solution to all our problems. It is the Holy Grail which, if recovered, will bring ultimate happiness.

This is a disastrous path, for we are expecting romance to give us something that only religion is designed to offer. When we begin to worship romantic love, it collapses under the weight.

—*Alan Loy McGinnis*

Don't Stand Idly By

Scripture Reading: Matthew 25:14-30
Key Verse: Matthew 25:21

> *Well done, good and faithful servant!*

———— ✍ ————

A lobster, when left high and dry among the rocks, doesn't have sense and energy enough to work his way back to the sea, but waits for the sea to come to him. If it doesn't come, he remains where he is and dies, although the slightest exertion would have enabled him to reach the waves, which are perhaps tossing and tumbling within a yard of him.

There is likewise a tide in human affairs that casts people into tight places, and leaves them there like stranded lobsters. If they choose to lie where the breakers have thrown them, expecting some great billow to take them on its big shoulders and carry them to smooth water, the chances are that their hopes will never be realized.

In today's passage God calls us to faithfully use our talents for Him, and He warns those who do not use the talents He has given them. Now consider what God is saying specifically to you in this parable that Jesus told.

What talents has God given you? Too often we think of talents as fully developed abilities, but it is only as we cultivate our talents that they become mature. Further-more, we must be willing to take the risk of using our talents. When we do, we then find out how far God can take us. Many times people will give you indications of what your talents are: "You're a good teacher; you write such comforting notes; when I'm in trouble you're always there; your singing really lifts me up!" Listen to what people are encouraging you about, since this could be God's way of telling you of that special gift He has given you.

Let's look at today's Scripture. In this parable the first two servants were willing to take a risk. Not only did they receive a 100 percent return for their efforts, but their master said, "Well done, good and faithful servant! You have been faithful with a few things; I will put you in charge of many things. Come and share your master's happiness!" (Matthew 25:21,22). Note that despite their different talents and abilities the first two servants received the same reward, indicating that God requires us to be faithful in the use of our abilities, whatever they are.

If you want to be successful in God's eyes, you must first be faithful with a few things. Then God will put you in charge of many things. Do you think no one could be blessed by your talent? This passage tells you to take the risk. Volunteer for that position, write that book, sign up for that class, offer to help with that project. Listen to God today as He calls you to the life of adventure that comes with using the gifts He has given you. Don't limit God.

Now let's look at the warning to those of us who don't use our talents. The third servant was afraid. Unwilling to take a risk with his one talent, he went and buried it in the ground. Are you burying your talents? God will hold you responsible for what you do with your talents, with your life. This third servant is condemned for his slothfulness and indifference.

God wants you to take the risk of using the talents He has given you, even if they don't seem like much to you. Take the first step today and you'll be amazed at what God can do with ordinary people. And you'll also be blessed when one day you stand before God and hear Him say, "Well done, good and faithful servant!"

Prayer

> *Father God, at times we don't feel we have any talents. You said You have given each of Your children special gifts. Today we're asking You for Your direction. Lord, how do You want us to use our talents for Your glory? Thank You for listening to our prayer. Help us hear Your answer. Amen.*

Taking Action

- Ask God today to reveal to you as a couple those special gifts that He wants you to develop.

- Ask a friend to share with you his perception of your special gifts or talents.

- Develop a plan and a timetable to begin using these talents and gifts for the Lord.

- Step out and serve someone today (start with your mate and family).

Reading On

Exodus 4:10-12   Ephesians 3:14-21
Ephesians 5:21

It All Starts at Home

Scripture Reading: Psalm 127:1–128:4

Key Verse: Psalm 127:3

> *Sons are a heritage from the Lord, children a reward from him.*

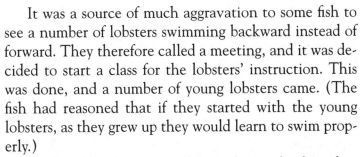

It was a source of much aggravation to some fish to see a number of lobsters swimming backward instead of forward. They therefore called a meeting, and it was decided to start a class for the lobsters' instruction. This was done, and a number of young lobsters came. (The fish had reasoned that if they started with the young lobsters, as they grew up they would learn to swim properly.)

At first they did very well, but afterward, when they returned home and saw their fathers and mothers swimming in the old way, they soon forgot their lessons.

So it is that many a child well taught at school drifts backward by a bad home influence.

In a recent Bible study that we attended, the teacher asked us, "Did you feel loved by your parents when you were a child?" The answers were disturbing and, for us parents, quite convicting.

- "Dad took us on trips, but he played golf all the time we were away."
- "Mom was too involved at the country club to spend time with us."
- "They were too busy for me."
- "A lot of pizzas were delivered to our house on Friday nights when my parents went out for the evening."
- "I spent too much time with the babysitters."
- "I got in their way. I wasn't important to them."
- "Mom didn't have to work, but she did so she wouldn't have to be home with us children."

What do you think your children would say if someone asked them, "Do you feel loved by your parents?" Which of your actions would support their answer, positive or negative?

Today's Scripture reading gives us some principles for building a family in which children are confident that their parents love them. First, the psalmist addresses the foundation and protection of the home: "Unless the Lord builds the house, its builders labor in vain. Unless the Lord watches over the city, the watchmen stand guard in vain" (verse 1). The protective wall surrounding a city was the very first thing to be constructed when a new city was built. The people of the Old Testament knew they needed protection from the enemy, but they were also smart enough to know that walls could be climbed over, knocked down, or broken apart. They realized that their ultimate security was the Lord standing guard over the city.

Are you looking to God to help you build your home? Are you trusting the Lord to be the guard over your family? Many forces in today's society threaten the family. When we drive the Southern California freeways, we see parents who are burning the candle at both ends to provide for all the material things they think will make their families happy.

We rise early and retire late, but Psalm 127:2 tells us that these efforts are futile. We are to do our best to provide for and protect our family, but we must trust first and foremost in God to take care of them.

In verse three we read that "children are a reward [gift] from [the Lord]." In the Hebrew, "gift" means "property," "possession." Truly God has loaned us our children to care for and to enjoy for a certain period of time. They remain His property, His possessions. As stewards of our children we are to take care of them, and that takes time.

We love to grow vegetables each summer, and are always amazed at what it takes to get a good crop. We have to cultivate the soil, sow the seeds, water, fertilize, weed, and prune. Raising children takes a lot of time, care, nurturing, and cultivating too. We can't neglect these responsibilities if we are going to produce good fruit. Left to themselves, our children—like the garden—will fail to seed and will grow, if anything, only weeds. When I *do* tend the garden, however, I'm rewarded by corn, tomatoes, cucumbers, and beans. Just as the harvest is my reward, so God-fearing children are a parent's reward.

Next, comparing children to arrows in the hands of a warrior, Psalm 127:4,5 talks about how parents are to handle their offspring. Wise and skillful parents will know their children, understand them, and carefully point them in the right direction before shooting them into the world. And, as you may have learned in an archery class, shooting an arrow straight and hitting a target is a lot harder in real life than it looks like in the movies or on TV. Likewise, godly and skillful parenting isn't easy.

The last section of today's selection teaches the importance of the Lord's presence in the home.

- The Lord is central to a home's happiness (Psalm 128:1,2).
- A wife who knows the Lord will be a source of beauty and life in the home (Psalm 128:3a).
- With the Lord's blessing, children will flourish like olive trees, which generously provide food, oil, and shelter for others (Psalm 128:3b).

What can you as a couple do to make the Lord's presence more recognizable in your home?

Finally, to ask a more pointed question, what kind of steward are you being in your home? God has entrusted to you some very special people—your children. You will be held accountable for how you take care of them. But you're not in it alone. God offers guidelines like those we looked at today plus His wisdom and His love, to help you do the job and do it well.

Prayer

> *Father God, forgive us for the ways we short-change our children. Help us know how to slow down the pace of life. Help us stay very aware that our children will be with us for just a short time, and that how we treat them will affect them and their children's lives too. Continue to teach us how to be the parents You want us to be. Amen.*

Taking Action

- "Our attitude toward our children reveals our attitude toward God." What does this statement mean to you?

- When you're talking to your children today, make a point of looking right into their eyes as you listen.

- Where do you need to be more consistent in teaching your children what is right and what is wrong?

- Give your child the gift of time—today and every day.

- Have you ever camped out inside? This weekend, go camping in your family room. Get your sleeping bags and a flashlight. Make shadow animals on the walls and ceilings. Review your week and plan something for the future. And don't forget the popcorn and hot chocolate.

Reading On

James 1:19,20   Proverbs 18:10
Matthew 18:5,6   Proverbs 16:24

Stop thinking of your marriage partner's relatives as a special breed known as in-laws (a term with faintly unpleasant connotations) and think of them simply as human beings with flaws and imperfections but also lovable qualities. Just discard the in-law label in your mind. Think of them as people. Treat them like people!

—*Ruth Stafford Peale*

If We Knock Together, We Sink Together

Scripture Reading: Mark 3:24-27

Key Verse: Mark 3:25

> *If a house is divided against itself, that house cannot stand.*

If two ships of the same squadron are scattered from each other by a storm, how can they come to the relief of each other? If they clash together, will not the one endanger the other and herself too? An old Dutch saying of two earthen pots floating together on the water was: "If we knock together, we sink together."

The early sailors knew very well the truth of keeping ships from clashing together. Many captains wished they didn't bang together and sink to the bottom of the ocean with ship, crew, and cargo.

Today the family unit is under great stress, and many families are falling victim to separation and knocking together. Because of this we find victims lying by the wayside due to the powerful force of Satan.

Abraham Lincoln said when he accepted the nomination for a United States Senate seat, "Either the opponents of slavery will arrest the further spread of it and place it where the public mind shall rest in the belief that it is in the course of ultimate extinction, or its advocates will push it forward till it shall become alike lawful in all the states, old as well as new—north as well as south."

Lincoln's stand against slavery and for the equality of all people resulted in his defeat in the election, but Lincoln responded philosophically: "Though I now sink out of view and shall be forgotten, I believe I have made some marks which will tell for the cause of civil liberty long after I am gone." Well, Lincoln certainly didn't "sink out of view"! As President of the United States he worked to bring together those who had been at war and to heal the hurts that had divided the nation and even some families within it.

Many families today are divided and need to be brought together; many hurts in those families need to be healed. We have watched this happen in our own extended family. Two of our aunts, who were sisters, hadn't spoken to each other for ten years. The initial disagreement, as slight as it may have been, became unbridgeable. Neither would apologize or admit to being wrong. Having watched this go on for a long time, Emilie decided that she was going to be the peacemaker. She arranged a family gathering and invited both aunts together. After just a short time, the two began to open up and talk to each other. By the end of the evening they had made amends, and they were able to enjoy the last 15 years of their lives together.

Maybe such division exists in your family. If so, know that the warning in today's Scripture is for you: "If a house is divided against itself, that house cannot stand." If a family remains divided, it will collapse. What can you do to help bring unity to your family? What can you do to help healing come to your home? Whatever steps you decide to take, know that you'll need much patience and many prayers. As you seek God's blessing on your attempts to rebuild your home, ask Him to give you wisdom and understanding. Know, too, that it will take time to rebuild what has been destroyed by division; don't feel that it must be resolved quickly. Be willing to walk by faith, not by sight, and pray earnestly for healing each step of the way.

Prayer

> *Father God, use us to be a healer in our family. Use us to help bring unity where there is now division. Show us the steps to take. We thank You that You will be with us and our family members as we try to build bridges and learn to forgive one another. Amen.*

Taking Action

- Where in your family is there division? Where is there a need for healing and reunification? What one person could you start focusing your prayers on?

- Ask your spouse to join you in praying about this person and the goal of unity within the family.

- Develop a plan for reuniting this family member with the family and then take the risky step of putting that plan into action.

Reading On

Matthew 12:25-27   Luke 11:17-22

Agape love enriches our family ties, our national ties, our ethnic ties. Agape love makes us more sensitive to the wonder of the world around us and to the various people who enter our lives. Agape love even makes us more intimate with those in the very inner circle. Agape makes us better lovers. Its fundamental acceptance of the person next to us enriches eros. It completes beauty and intimacy.

—*Earl F. Palmer*

Love with Heart, Soul, and Strength

Scripture Reading: Deuteronomy 6:4-9
Key Verse: Deuteronomy 6:5

> Love the Lord your God with all your heart and with all your soul and with all your strength.

———— ☙ ————

Today's Scripture, along with Matthew 22:34-40, talks about three basic loves—love of God, love of neighbor, and love of self. What a difference we Christians would make in the world if we were able to love in this way! The Deuteronomy passage goes on and challenges us to:

- put these commandments in our hearts;
- impress them on our children;
- talk about them continually;
- "tie them as symbols" on our bodies;
- write them on our door frames and gates.

Clearly, this command to love is important to God.
But as we try to remain constantly aware of God's command, *how do we live out these three loves?* In his letter

to the Ephesian church, Paul helps us to answer that question by saying, "Be filled with the Spirit" (Ephesians 5:18).

If we are loving ourselves, we will speak and sing words of joy: "Speak to one another with psalms, hymns and spiritual songs. Sing and make music in your heart to the Lord" (verse 19). Satisfied lives will be ones of joy, praise, and excitement. They will reflect positive thoughts, ideas, and praises to God. What a great test to see where our personal satisfaction is! Are we known as a person who is fun to be around or as someone who people avoid? God wants us to be satisfied with ourselves through Christ and reflect the joy of the Lord in our soul, mind, and spirit.

If we are loving God, we will be able to fulfill the command of Ephesians 5:20 by "always giving thanks for all things in the name of our Lord Jesus Christ to God, even the Father" (NASB). If we love God, we will find ourselves giving thanks for all things. We will have an appreciative heart for all that goes on around us. Positive words will flow from our lips unto God.

If we are loving other people, we will be able to "be subject to one another in the fear of Christ" (verse 21 NASB). When we truly love God we become equipped to be submissive to others. These word "subject" or "submissive" have taken a beating in today's culture. In essence, these words are telling us to be satisfied with other people to the point that we are willing to step aside in our personal relationships. We are willing to allow another person's needs to take precedence over our own. The submission is to be based on reverence for God. It is impossible to be subject to one another by human desire. It is possible only when we mutually submit to one another out of respect for God.

Together, the commands to love God with all our heart, all our soul, and all our strength, and to love God, others, and ourselves are a call to put first things first. And it is a daily challenge to do so.

Prayer

Father God, You know the demands on us as a couple. Help us to meet these challenges by starting each day with the question, "What can I do to love God with all my heart, soul, and strength?" Help our relationships with others to fall into place as I make loving You and loving them my goal. And help us to better understand what kind of love You want us to have for ourselves. Your call to love seems so basic, but we know we'll be working at it our whole lives. Amen.

Taking Action

*   Write down several ways you presently live out your love of:
      —God
      —others
      —self.

Now write down several new ways to love God, others, and yourself. Choose one in each category to start doing this week:
      —God
      —others
      —self.

Reading On

Ephesians 5:18-21   Matthew 22:36-40

Work Through Me Gentleness

My family lives with a father and husband who is still too rigid. When Ann calls for dinner and I leave my very significant activity, I expect the food to be on the table ready to serve. Quite often it's still in the process. "Now who does she think she is—keeping his eminence waiting?" And when I'm in my rigid mood, I sure let her know of the terrible inconvenience she has caused me! How would you like to live with someone like that?

Ann has a choice of response to my rigidity—anger, or love and acceptance. Her prayer at that moment can be "God, change that turkey so he'll be more pleasant to live with," or, "Lord, You are the grace I need now to forgive Ray, to love him and accept him as he is. Work through me the gentleness I need now to confront him lovingly with the rigidity which makes him unhappy."

Ann and I have covenanted that we will not ask God to change the other until He has finished using that particular irritation to "perfect" us. Ann would pray, "Lord, don't change Ray's rigidness until You are finished using it to reshape and build me."

—*Ray Burwick*

A Husband, a Gentle Warrior, and a Wife of Noble Character

Scripture Reading: Proverbs 12:1-7

Key Verse: Proverbs 12:4

> *A wife of noble character is her husband's crown, but a disgraceful wife is like decay in his bones.*

———— ✑ ————

Major Sullivan Ballou wrote this letter to his devoted wife, Sarah, a week before Manassas, the first battle of Bull Run. Sarah must have been a wife of noble character who truly was a crown to her soldier husband.

July 14, 1861
Camp Clerk, Washington, D.C.

My very dear Sarah,

The indications are very strong that we shall move in a few days—perhaps tomorrow. Lest I should not be able to write again, I feel impelled to write a few lines that may fall under your eye when I shall be no more. . . .

I have no misgivings about, or lack of confidence in, the cause in which I am engaged, and my courage does not halt or falter. I know how strongly American civilization now leans on the triumph of the Government, and how great a debt we owe to those who went before us through the blood and sufferings of the Revolution. And I am willing—perfectly willing—to lay down all my joys in this life to help maintain this Government and to pay that debt.

Sarah, my love for you is deathless; it seems to bind me with mighty cables that nothing but Omnipotence could break; and yet my love of Country comes over me like a strong wind and bears me unresistibly on with all these chains to the battlefield.

The memories of the blissful moments I have spent with you come creeping over me, and I feel most gratified to God and to you that I have enjoyed them so long. And hard it is for me to give them up and burn to ashes the hopes of future years, when, God willing, we might still have lived and loved together, and seen our sons grow up to honorable manhood around us. I have, I know, but few and small claims upon Divine Providence, but something whispers to me—perhaps it is the wafted prayer of my little Edgar, that I shall return to my loved ones unharmed. If I do not, my dear Sarah, never forget how much I love you, and when my last breath escapes me on the battlefield, it will whisper your name. Forgive my many faults, and the many pains I have caused you. How thoughtless and foolish I have oftentimes been! How gladly would I wash out with my tears every little spot upon your happiness. . . .

But, O Sarah! if the dead can come back to this earth and flit unseen around those they loved, I shall always be near you; in the gladdest days and in the darkest nights . . . *always, always*, and if there be a soft breeze upon your cheek, it shall be my breath; as the cool air fans your throbbing temple, it shall be my spirit passing by. Sarah, do not mourn me dead; think I am gone and wait for thee, for we shall meet again.[18]

Sullivan Ballou was killed at the first battle of Bull Run, but he had left his wife these few lines of love. She undoubtedly thought of her beloved husband whenever a soft breeze touched her cheek. Her husband had been both strong and sensitive, tough and tender. As his letter reflects, he faced death with courage, standing strong in his convictions and unwavering in his commitment to his country, his wife, and his God. And I would guess that some of his courage resulted from a wife who believed in him, encouraged him, and made him her hero.

Supporting your man will indeed encourage him to be the man—and husband and father—that God wants him to be. Like Sullivan Ballou, who was both tough and tender, your husband can come to know the strength of his masculinity. He can know the balance between strong and sensitive that God intended when He made man. I'm sure God looked down upon Major Ballou and said, "It was good." You can help your man earn those same words of praise and he will praise you at the gates.

May all of us as wives strive to be women of noble character and our husband's crown.

Prayer

Father God, we desire as a man to be a gentle warrior and as a woman to be of noble character. We want to find pleasure in Your sight and we want to be worthy to our mate. Please bring into our lives those people who will show us how to develop Christian character. May we be receptive to changes. We want them to know that we love them very much. In all situations we want to express love no matter what the circumstances or situations. Amen.

Taking Action

- Write a similar letter to each other not knowing what might happen to you in the next 40 hours.
- Mail your letters to each other.
- Risk and read each other's letters out loud. (Be ready to cry.)

Meditate on these:

- Find good men and women to emulate.
- Carry no grudges. They'll weigh you down.
- Every day look for some little thing you can do to improve your relationship to your spouse.

Reading On

Philippians 4:8   Romans 14:18,19
Ephesians 5:21

God Gives Us a New Song

Scripture Reading: Psalm 40:1-4

Key Verse: Psalm 40:3

> He put a new song in my mouth, a hymn of praise to our God.

———— ✑ ————

What would our life be without joy? Without joy, we can do nothing: We would be like a violin out of tune, which yields nothing but harsh sounds. Life without joy is like a bone out of joint, which doesn't function properly. We can do nothing well without joy.

God will give us a new song in our mouths and a hymn of praise to Him. When we come before God with an open heart and a voice of confession, He will forgive us of all unrighteousness (1 John 1:9). With this emptying of ourselves He will give us a new song—one written just for us.

As a family, we can take this promise and turn our joy and song into laughter. We are a country that has forgotten how to laugh. We greatly need people who have a good sense of humor between Mom, Dad, and the children. Bob Benson in his poem "Laughter in the Walls" captures the essence of spending time together in laughter as a family.

I pass a lot of houses on my way home—
some pretty,
         some expensive,
                  some inviting—
but my heart always skips a beat
         when I turn down the road
and see my house nestled against the hill.
         I guess I'm especially proud
of the house and the way it looks because
         I drew the plans myself.
It started out large enough for us—
         I even had a study—
two teenaged boys now reside in there.
         And it had a guest room—
my girl and nine dolls are permanent guests.
         It had a small room Peg
had hoped would be her sewing room—
         the two boys swinging on the Dutch door
have claimed this room as their own.
         So it really doesn't look right now
as if I'm much of an architect.
         But it will get larger again—
one by one they will go away
         to work,
                  to college,
         to service,
         to their own houses,
and then there will be room—
         a guest room,
                  a study,
         and sewing room
         for just the two of us.

But it won't be empty—
    every corner
        every room
        every nick
            in the coffee table
will be crowded with memories.
Memories of picnics,
    parties, Christmases,
    bedside vigils, summers,
    fires, winters, going barefoot,
leaving for vacation, cats,
    conversations, black eyes,
graduations, first dates,
    ball games, arguments,
washing dishes, bicycles,
    dogs, boat rides,
getting home from vacation,
    meals, rabbits and
a thousand other things
    that fill the lives
of those who would raise five.
    And Peg and I will sit
quietly by the fire
    and listen to the
    laughter in the walls.[19]

When the children are gone, when there are no lunches to be made, when retirement sets in—what will you hear in your walls? We pray it's laughter, for God created laughter. May your life truly reflect joy and laughter.

Prayer

Father God, let us take time to build precious memories with our family and friends. We are here for a very short while and then we are gone—gone from those who are so dear to us. How will we be remembered? As someone who is angry, screaming, bitter? Or as lovable, laughable, joyful people? May our laughter echo strong in the walls long after we're gone. Show us the way. Amen.

Taking Action

- Buy a clean joke book and tell a new joke at the dinner table each day for one week. Begin to laugh at home.

- Loan the book to another member of the family and let him or her tell a joke for each dinner meal next week.

- Realize that the children will only be home for a short period of your life. Create your own laughter in the walls.

- Rediscover and nurture the "child" inside of you. It's the key to your creativity, your sense of wonder and of joy.

Reading On

Habakkuk 3:17,18   Luke 15:9,10
Acts 2:46,47   1 Chronicles 29:9

Take my heart
  and make it
Your dwelling place
  so that everyone
I touch
  will be touched also
by You!

—*Alice Joyce Davidson*

Love Must
Be Sincere

Scripture Reading: Romans 12:9-21

Key Verse: Romans 12:9

> *Love must be sincere. Hate what is evil; cling to what is good.*

Dr. Halbeck, a missionary of the Church of England in the South of Africa, from the top of a neighboring hill saw lepers at work. He noticed two particularly, sowing peas in the field. One had no hands; the other had no feet, these members being wasted away by disease. The one who wanted the hands was carrying the other, who lacked the feet, upon his back; and he in turn carried the bag of seed, and dropped a pea every now and then, which the other pressed into the ground with his feet; and so they managed the work of one man between the two. Such should be the true union of the members of Christ's body, in which all the members should have the same care one for another."[20]

What a vivid and powerful picture of how the body of Christ is to function! Fundamental to that kind of unity is the love of Jesus. In today's reading we are called to have a love that is "sincere." In some translations Romans 12:9 reads, "Let love be without hypocrisy." The term "hypocrisy" is a stage term which means "acting a part." At the theater we see actors pretending to be characters who aren't at all what the actors are like in real life. But in our walk of faith, we who are Christians are not to pretend to be someone we're not. Our love for one another is to be sincere, not an act of hypocrisy.

In today's passage Paul gives other directives on how to live a Christian life that pleases and glorifies God. We are to choose the proper pathway in which to live, and some of these paths are outlined below:

The Path of Sincerity (verse 9):
- Love must be sincere.
- Hate what is evil.
- Cling to what is good.

The Path of Humility (verse 10):
- Be devoted to one another in brotherly love.
- Honor one another above ourselves.

The Path of Passion (verses 11,12):
- Never lack in zeal.
- Keep fervent about serving the Lord.
- Be joyful in hope.
- Be patient in affliction.
- Be faithful in prayer.

The Path of Relationships (verses 13-21):
- Share with God's people who are in need.

- Practice hospitality.
- Bless those who persecute you.
- Do not curse those who hate you.
- Rejoice with those who rejoice.
- Mourn with those who mourn.
- Live in harmony with one another.
- Do not be proud.
- Be willing to associate with people of low position.
- Do not be conceited.
- Do not repay anyone evil for evil.
- Do what is right in the eyes of the Lord.
- Do not take revenge.
- If your enemy is hungry, feed him.
- If he is thirsty, give him something to drink.
- Do not be overcome by evil, but overcome evil with good.

God wants us to do all these things. No wonder we struggle every day to live the kind of life He wants us to live! In order to put these specifics into practice, we must read Scripture and pray. Doing so helps us to stand strong against Satan, who would love to derail us from our goal of living a life that pleases and glorifies God.

Prayer

Father God, here we are. Use us for Your kingdom. Teach us Your way of love. Fill us with Your love so that we may be willing to carry a brother or sister who needs our help, and help us to receive Your love when we need to be carried. It's a privilege to be called Your child. May we live a life worthy of that calling, a life that truly glorifies You. Amen.

Taking Action

- Choose six of the directives from the above list. Beside each one, note what you are going to do today and this week to live it out.

- Now write those six directives on an index card and take it with you as a reminder of the goals you have set for yourself. Better yet, memorize these directives.

Reading On

Proverbs 6:16-19   Philippians 4:8

Letting Go

Scripture Reading: Psalm 37:1-6

Key Verse: Psalm 37:4

> *Delight yourself in the Lord and he will give you the desires of your heart.*

———————⟨✦⟩———————

If you are like us, there are many things to let go of and not to continue to hold onto. We hold onto the past—the memories of the good times when we were all young and happily married, had good jobs and good health, and the children were young. We remember the vacations in the mountains, a stroll along the beach, Christmas at Mom and Dad's. Yes, even memories of the bad times seem to hold us captive. But these memories seem to limit us. On occasion we find our minds so desperately concentrating on the past that we forget to enjoy the thrills of the present or the anticipation of the future.

We even find ourselves holding onto people. Our insecurities won't let us branch out to meet new friends. In this ever-changing world, it seems like it is more difficult to get to know new people. We need to remind ourselves to risk new relationships. But instead we try desperately to be a blessing to our old friends that we have prayed with, laughed with, cried with, vacationed with, and endured transitions with between children and the empty nest. But we know we must let go of those fond friendships so we can be free to expand our friendship base. We need to make room for new relationships.

All of these "let go" desires are keeping us bundled up in the past (even though they were wonderful times). We pray that God will show us how to let go and move on. We need strength and courage to let go of those memories (though we love traditions and memories) so we can experience the fullness of this day and all the tomorrows that God has for us. We pray that God will let us step out in faith to do the things which are ours today and in the future.

The past is not always the only crippler. Often the anticipation of tomorrow can also bind us up to ineffectiveness. Depending upon our past experiences, we might find ourselves kidnapped by the dreams or desires for things to come. This vision may be limited because we have not revised those five-year-old goals. We need to stay fresh with new desires for the future. We don't have to do the future as we have done the past. We need to be open to God's new instructions and His fresh guidance with each breath we take.

Letting go may not be easy, but we know that with God's help we can let go and let Him work in our lives.

As found in Genesis 2:24, we need to let go of our children. This often is the most difficult "let go" we have in life.

Many years ago on "Focus on the Family," Dr. Dobson read a now famous "let go" letter on his daily radio program.

Dear Paul:

This is the most important letter I have ever written to you, and I hope you will take it as seriously as it is intended. I have given a great amount of thought and prayer to the matter I want to convey, and believe I am right in what I've decided to do.

For the past several years, you and I have been involved in a painful tug-of-war. You have been struggling to free yourself of my values and my wishes for your life. At the same time, I have been trying to hold you to what we both know is right. Even at the risk of nagging, I have been saying, "Go to church," "Choose the right friends," "Make good grades in school," "Prepare wisely for your future," etc. I'm sure you've gotten tired of this urging and warning, but I have only wanted the best for you. This is the only way I knew to keep you from making some of the mistakes so many others have made.

However, I've thought all of this over during the last months and I believe that my job as your father is now finished. Since the day you were born, I have done my best to do what was right for you. I have not always been successful—I've made mistakes and I've failed in many ways. Someday you will learn how difficult it is to be a good parent, and perhaps then you'll understand me better than you do now. But there's one area where I have never wavered: I've loved you with everything that is within me. It is impossible to convey the depth of my love for you through these years, and that affection is as great today as it's ever been. I will continue to be there in the future, although our relationship will change from this moment. As of now, you are free! You may reject God or accept Him, as you choose. Ultimately, you will answer only to Him, anyway. You may marry whomever you wish without protest from me. You may go to U.C.L.A. or U.S.C. or any other college of your selection. You may fail or succeed in each of life's responsibilities. The umbilical cord is broken.

I am not saying these things out of bitterness or anger. I still care what happens to you and am concerned for your welfare. I will pray for you daily, and if you come to me for advice, I'll offer my opinion. *But the responsibility now shifts from my shoulders to yours.* You are a man now, and you're entitled to make your own decisions—regardless of the consequences. Throughout your life I've tried to build a foundation of values which would prepare you for this moment of manhood and independence. That time has come, and my record is in the books.

I have confidence in you, son. You are gifted and have been blessed in so many ways. I believe God will lead you and guide your footsteps, and I am optimistic about the future. Regardless of the outcome, I will always have a special tenderness in my heart for my beloved son.

Dad

Each family is unique in how it releases its children into adulthood and marriage. In the Jewish wedding ceremonies we have attended, parents of the bride and groom recite vows releasing their children from parental authority. This might be a good tradition to add to our Christian ceremony. Formally releasing our children can serve to eliminate a lot of guilt—in us and our kids—which often attends a child's departure to marry.

We often cling to our children because we fear they are exiting our lives completely. But departure doesn't mean that we will no longer see them, have them over for dinner, or counsel them when they seek it. But it does mean that we no longer try to control them as we did when they were younger.

Prayer

> *Father God, You know that we struggle with the "letting go" of many precious memories, relationships, possessions, health, loved ones, and good friends. Life is always in motion—it doesn't stand still. Please teach us to appreciate all the things You have given us in life, but also let us be sensitive to the realities of the future. Give us the desire, the strength, and the courage to move on in life. Let us be flexible in this ever-changing world. Thank You for hearing our prayers of release. Amen.*

Taking Action

- Write down in your journal three things you are going to let go. How are you going to do this? An action, a telephone call, a letter, a prayer?

- Write down in your journal three new adventures that will take their place. How will you implement these new adventures?

Reading On

Proverbs 3:5,6   Matthew 6:31,32
1 Peter 5:7   Psalm 40:4

From Good Parents Come Good Children

Scripture Reading: Matthew 7:15-20

Key Verse: Matthew 7:18

> *A good tree cannot bear bad fruit, and a bad tree cannot bear good fruit.*

In this passage for today, the writer is talking in agricultural terms about trees, fruit, and how fruit comes about. He is stressing to the reader that we are to discern the people we meet by looking at the fruit they bear. He is also stressing that we ourselves are known by the fruit we bear, and that our fruit should be good.

As good parents we are continually challenged by raising good children—not chemists, not computer whizzes, not star athletes, but good children. Many of us spend so much of our time raising a good _____ that we don't think much about teaching moral and ethical values.

Woodrow Wilson, while president of Princeton University, addressed an assembly of parents of the student body. Part of his speech was addressed to this very topic. In part he said that he received many letters from parents about their children. They wanted to know why the faculty couldn't make more out of the students and why they couldn't do more for them.

Mr. Wilson went on to give reasons why this wasn't always possible. He wanted the assembly to know that he wasn't trying to shock them or to be rude, but the main reason the school couldn't do what they were requesting was because the students were offspring of the parents. They were reared in the parents' homes, blood of their blood and bone of their bone. They had absorbed the ideas of their homes. The parents had formed and fashioned them.

We all want our children to do better than we have done. We want them to enjoy a higher standard of living than they have experienced in our homes (no matter how great that experience might have been). But as parents we often don't realize that a child will rarely display a higher standard of ambition, virtue, character, or godliness than that which is reflected by the parents.

As parents we can't expect someone else to do a better job with our children than we have done. We are the true educators of our children; all others are merely part of the supporting cast.

One of the Hebrew words for parent is "teacher." In today's culture we are all too willing to turn over the spiritual matters of our children to a pastor or Sunday school teacher, the sex education to a public school educator, the character-building to a coach, and the finances to a business instructor at school.

We are accountable to God to raise our children according to sound biblical principles. Let's not be so ready to farm these truths to outside agencies. We are the teachers and must never give up that responsibility, no matter how busy we become in life.

Prayer

Father God, You know how much we as parents want to raise good children. We want to have the blessing that Scripture talks about in Psalm 127:3-5. Give us as a couple the desire to be accountable to You for our children. We don't want to pawn off this responsibility to other agencies. We pray that our children will be helpful to us as needy parents, that they will be obedient to Your Word, that they will have teachable spirits toward our leadership. Give us a heart's desire to be teachers of our children. Amen.

Taking Action

- List in your journal five godly characteristics which you would like for each of your children to possess when they become 11 years old, 13 years old, and 18 years old.

- As a couple, what experiences and activities can you give them to learn each of these characteristics?

- Pray for each of your children today. Tell them individually that you love them. Give each a big hug and a kiss.

- Are your children fortunate to live in your home? Why?

Reading On

Acts 16:31	Isaiah 54:13
Proverbs 17:6	Psalm 128:3

Memories of the Garden Bench

Scripture Reading: Philippians 1:3-11
Key Verse: Philippians 1:3

I thank my God every time I remember you.

———————— ☙ ————————

To see a world in a grain of sand and a heaven in a wild flower; hold infinity in the palm of your hand, and eternity in an hour.
—William Blake, *Auguries of Innocence*

It was a warm sunny day for January in Riverside, California. Two of our five grandchildren were helping us enjoy this fine day. Ten-year-old Christine was helping her Grammy Em plan and cook the dinner. She was picking flowers to arrange for our dinner table. PaPa Bob and Bevan were raking the garden and picking oranges, avocados, and lemons off our trees that surround our property.

As the afternoon progressed, our working men became warm and tired.

Christine said, "Grammy, let's have tea." That's all it takes for me to stop whatever I'm doing and put the kettle on for Christine and me to have tea! In the process, we poured the men a tall glass of fresh juice on ice and prepared some yummy-for-the-tummy snacks. We carried the treats up the hill to PaPa and Bevan. How happy they were to receive the refreshment! They thanked us and headed for the bench that sits under a large shady avocado tree overlooking the grounds and our quaint, tree-lined little Rumsey Drive which winds by our barn.

As Christine and I left them, we headed back toward the house. Christine took my hand and said, "Grammy, I love you." "I love you too, Christine," I said.

I prepared the teakettle, and Christine pulled down the teapot and put the teacups on the table with our special silver teaspoons. We toasted thick sourdough bread that we spread with jam and butter. It was an instant tea party—just Christine and me.

That night as my Bob and I crawled in bed, we began to share about our day with the oh-so-wonderful grandchildren.

"What do a PaPa and seven-year-old grandson talk about on the bench under the big avocado tree?" I asked.

"Oh, very special things," Bob replied. "Boys talk just like you girls talk."

I could still picture PaPa Bob and seven-year-old Bevan—with smudges of dirt on both their faces—sitting on that bench.

Bob continued, "I told Bevan, 'Someday, Bevan, when PaPa's in heaven and you drive down Rumsey Drive as a man, you'll look at this bench we are sitting on and you can remember the day that Grammy Em and sister Christine served us jam and toast with a glass of juice.' Then Bevan said, 'Not only will I remember, but I will bring my son and someday he will bring his son and point to the bench and tell him about the toast and jam we ate on the bench under that big avocado tree over there.'"

How does a little boy understand and think through the process of generations?

How blessed we are to have the God-given opportunity to teach our children and grandchildren about the beauty of God's creations, about life and death, and most of all about God the Father, God the Son, and God the Holy Spirit.

Take time out of that busy schedule of yours and create a moment to remember forever! It could be with your spouse, a child, a grandchild, or a friend. Give your time to them that says, "You are important." All the busyness of life can stop for a short time. The serenity will be good for you. Our hearts and souls cry out to us, "Please stop and let me rest; I'm so tired of the high-tech society that begs for more; enough is enough."

The ever-increasing noises are emotional storms to our body; they take our energy, scare us, and blur our vision for the future. We all want peace, stillness, and memories that give us purpose.

Your memory may not be the garden bench, but somewhere there is an altar where you can plant a memory that will last a lifetime.

Prayer

Father God, we think we only live for today, but Scripture tells us to look to the future and eternity. The world wants us to conform to the pressures of the here-and-now and focus on the temporal. Help us to take time to develop a future orientation for myself and our family. What You have done for us in the past gives us hope for the future. Amen.

Taking Action

- Take a child's hand. Take a walk and talk to each other.
- Give a cup of refreshment to someone today—a cup of tea or a glass of juice.
- Tell someone, "I love you."
- Call a friend on the phone to tell him or her what your past memory of him has meant to you.
- Tell God how much you appreciate the memories that have been created by the words of Scripture.

Reading On

1 Corinthians 1:4   Deuteronomy 6:6,7
Psalm 67:1   Romans 12:2

Contentment— The Secret of Life

Scripture Reading: 1 Timothy 6:1-10
Key Verse: 1 Timothy 6:6

Godliness with contentment is great gain.

———————⟨𝒫⟩———————

A bishop of the early Church who was a remarkable example of contentment was asked his secret. The old man replied, "It consists in nothing more than making a right use of my eyes. In whatever circumstance I am, I first of all look up to heaven and remember that my principal business here is to get there; I then look down upon the earth, and remember how small a place I shall occupy in it when I die and am buried; I then look abroad in the world and observe what multitudes there are who are in all respects more unhappy than myself. Thus I learn where true happiness is placed, where all our cares must end, and what little reason I have to complain."

We all know of people who are always complaining about their situation: "If only we had a bigger home; if only we had a better car; I won't be happy until we move back to _____; this physical handicap is holding me back; we need to bring home at least 200 dollars more a month."

Conditions and situations will never be perfect. We have become a culture which is always focusing on perfect conditions, but if we wait for perfection to be content we will never be happy. *Things* do not bring us contentment. It only comes about when, as a couple, we focus upon why we are here on this earth and then begin to live out this purpose.

One of our famous sayings is, "If you're not content with what you have, you'll never be content with what you want." We meet many people who are always looking to the future—the next paycheck, the next home, the next church, the next month, the next school, and, in some cases, the next marriage partner. We are a country characterized by discontent. Do you find yourself being drawn in to this mind-set?

Recently we were visiting our grandchild, Bradley Joe Barnes II. As we were holding him, rubbing our hands through his hair, tracing the shape of his toes and fingers, our minds started thinking about what he was going to be as he grew to manhood. Was he going to have good grades and go to college? Would he be a fireman, a pastor, a teacher, a coach, a salesman? Suddenly we realized that we were thinking about *what* he could be rather than focusing our thoughts and prayers on *who* he would be.

In today's culture we are all drawn away from spiritual pursuits to putting our hope in wealth (1 Timothy 6:17) and to building our lives around ways to accomplish this ambition. As we sat there in Bradley Joe's room, we began praying that all of his extended family might teach him higher values than money, career, and fame. Not that these are evil, but the value we place on them can lead to our downfall (1 Timothy 6:9).

In today's passage Paul states, "Godliness with contentment is great gain" (1 Timothy 6:6). When we find ourselves looking to the future because we aren't content with today, may God give us a peace of mind that lets us rest where He has placed us. Be content today!

Prayer

Father God, You know that my heart's desire is to be content in whatever state I'm in. I want to be like Paul in that regard. You have given me so much and I want to graciously thank You for those blessings. Amen.

Taking Action

- Instead of being discontent with your station in life, start praising God for where you are.
- Ask God to reveal to you what you can learn in your present situation.
- Write a letter to God thanking Him for all your blessings. Name them individually.

Reading On

1 Timothy 6:11-21   Proverbs 22:1,2
Mark 10:17-25

God Did Promise

If I could, I'd write for you a rainbow
And splash it with all the colors of God
And hang it in the window of your being
So that each new God's morning
Your eyes would open first to Hope and
    Promise.
If I could, I'd wipe away your tears
And hold you close forever in shalom.
But God never promised
I could write a rainbow,
Never promise I could suffer for you,
Only promised I could love you.
That I do.

—*Ann Weems*

A Lesson in Prayer

Scripture Reading: Colossians 1:9-12

Key Verse: Colossians 1:9

> *Since the day we heard about you, we have not stopped praying for you and asking God to fill you with the knowledge of his will through all spiritual wisdom and understanding.*

———————⊘———————

A number of ministers were assembled for the discussion of difficult questions. Among others, the question was asked how the command to "pray without ceasing" could be complied with. Various suppositions were given, and eventually one of the ministers was appointed to write an essay on the subject to be read at the next meeting.

Overheard by a female servant, she exclaimed, "What! A whole month waiting to find the meaning of that text? It is one of the easiest and best texts in the Bible."

"Well, well!" replied an old minister. "Mary, what can you say about it? Let us know how you understand it. Can you pray all the time?" "Oh, yes, sir!" "What? When you have so many things to do?" "Why, sir, the more I have to do, the more I can pray!" "Indeed! Well, Mary, let us know how you do this."

"Well, sir," she replied, "when I first open my eyes in the morning, I pray, 'Lord, open the eyes of my understanding'; while I'm dressing I pray that I may be clothed with the robe of righteousness; when I have washed I ask for the washing of regeneration; as I begin to work I pray that I may have strength equal to my day; when I begin to kindle the fire I pray that God's work may revive in my soul; as I sweep out the house I pray that my heart may be cleansed from all its impurities; while preparing and eating breakfast I desire to be fed with the hidden manna and the sincere milk of the Word; as I am busy with the children I look up to God as my Father and pray for the spirit of adoption, that I may be His child; and so on all day. Everything I do furnishes me with a thought for prayer."

"Enough, enough!" cried the old minister; "these things are revealed to babes, and often hid from the wise and prudent. Go on, Mary," he continued; "pray without ceasing; and as for us, my brethren, let us bless the Lord for this exposition and remember that He has said, 'The meek will he guide in judgment.'"

After this little event the essay was not considered necessary.[21]

Prayer is so important in our daily lives. As this young Mary was able to pray all through the day, we are to pray specifically for our friends. There is no more important friendship than that between a husband and wife in marriage.

Start each day and end each evening in a prayer of thanksgiving for a new day (morning) and for the provisions of the day (evening).

As we spend time with God, we open ourselves to His work in our hearts and in our lives. Then, as we see Him working, we will want to know Him even more. We will want our prayer life to be all that it can be. What does that mean? How should we be praying?

In Scripture we find many models of prayer, and probably foremost is the Lord's Prayer (Matthew 6:9-13). This wonderful example includes important elements of prayer. We find words of adoration, of submission to God's will, of petition, and of praise. We can learn much from the model our Lord gave when His disciples said, "Teach us to pray" (Luke 11:1).

As meaningful as the Lord's Prayer is to us, we have also found Colossians 1:9-12 to be a powerful guide in our prayer life. If you aren't in the habit of praying or if you want to renew your time with God, we challenge you to read this passage of Scripture every day for 30 days. Look at it in small pieces, dwell on its message each day, and take action upon what it says; you'll become a new person.

Read today's Scripture passage again and think about how wonderful a prayer it is for you to pray for your mate and your friends. Knowing that a friend is praying for you is a real source of encouragement and support. If you aren't praying for your mate and friends daily, let us suggest that Colossians 1:9-12 be your model. Look at what you'll be asking God:

- That your mate and your friends will have the spiritual wisdom and understanding they need to know God's will.

- That they will "walk in a manner worthy of the Lord, to please Him in all respects" (verse 10 NASB).
- That your mate and friends will be bearing "fruit in all good work and increasing in the knowledge of God" (verse 10 NASB).
- That they will be "strengthened with all power . . . for the attaining of all steadfastness and patience" (verse 11 NASB).

You can end your prayer by joyously giving thanks to God for all He has given you (verse 12).

Did you hear those words? What an armor of protection and growth you can give your mate and friends with a prayer like that! With these powerful words and the Lord at their side, they will be able to deal with the challenges they face.

We also encourage you to tell your friends that you are praying for them each day, and if they are receptive, tell them the specifics of your prayers for them. Let us assure you that it is a real comfort to have friends praying for you, asking God to give wisdom and understanding, to enable you to honor Him in all you do, to help you bear fruit for His kingdom, and to grant you strength, steadfastness, and patience.

Know too that these verses from Colossians are a good model for your prayers for other members of your family, your neighbors, and yourself. After all, all of God's people need to know His will, to honor Him in everything they do, to grow in the knowledge of the Lord, and to be strong, steadfast, and patient as they serve Him.

Prayer

Father God, let us as a couple know how to pray for our mates, our friends, and our family. Let us take the time to study, for prayer enables us to be stronger in our walk with You. We are open to Your teaching and we want to learn. Amen.

Taking Action

- In your journals write down the names of your spouse and one to three friends that you want to pray for each day. Under each name list several specific areas which you want to pray about for them.

- Read Colossians 1:9-12 for 30 straight days. Think specifically of the friends you listed in your journal.

Reading On

Ephesians 3:14-19   Philemon 4-7

Friendship is a risk. There are usually no advance warnings about potential hazards. Sometimes I have no idea what's in the package but I reach out and take it anyhow, because God has created me for giving and receiving love. Any other way is far too lonely. But sometimes friendship's gift may contain perils, crises, transformations, complications I didn't count on in the beginning. What then?

I go right on loving and caring, but I learn that loving sometimes makes hard demands. Sometimes friendship withholds. Sometimes friendship must wound and wean for the health and wholeness of the other person—for the sake of balance.

—*Ruth Senter*

Our Source of Love
and Friendship

Scripture Reading: 1 Corinthians 13:4-13

Key Verse: 1 Corinthians 13:4

Love is patient, love is kind. It does not envy,
it does not boast, it is not proud.

———— ⊘ ————

Several years ago our friend Bill Thornburgh was diagnosed with leukemia. Eighteen months and three rounds of chemotherapy treatment later, Bill went home to be with the Lord. Soon afterward, while his wife Carole was getting ready to visit Bill's sister, she decided to take some of Bill's old books. While sorting through them she found an envelope addressed to her from Bill. He had written Carole an Easter card two years earlier, and she had tucked it away in a book. Rediscovering the card, she thanked God for her husband's written words.

At Christmastime, Carole had this Easter message from her husband:

A Tearful Week
A Long Week
A Hard Week
A Lonely Week

A Painful Week
A Revealing Week
A Recovering Week
A Reassuring Week
A Peace Week
A Rededication Week
A Friendship Week
A Love Week
A Roller Coaster Week
A Renewal Week
A Glorious Week
A Victorious Week
A Life Changing Week
But A Week I Will Never Lose Sight Of
May God be our source of true love and friendship. You
have been so good these days. I love you for it. You
have been all a husband would desire. Forgive me,
Sweet, for not keeping our love fresh. I love you.
Happy Easter and Happy Beginnings,
Bill

Bill's words offered Carole a comforting sense of his
presence after he was gone. But even when he was alive,
Bill and Carole spoke openly of their love for each other.
Do you and your wife? Don't wait until it's too late.

We husbands would do well to learn the language of
love. We need to practice saying "I love you." We need to
say those words, but we also need to speak them through
our sensitivity to our spouse, through our actions, and
through our conversation.

If I'm going to run some errands, for instance, I can
ask Emilie if there's anything I can get for her while I'm
out. I can let her know I'm listening to her by turning

off the television or putting down the paper. I can also show her I love her with an evening at the theater, a new dress, a gift certificate for a dress, a pair of shoes, a massage, or a weekend minivacation at one of her favorite retreats.

However I choose to show my love, I say aloud to Emilie, "Just another way to say 'I love you!'" Acts of kindness like this are powerful and effective ways to strengthen your friendship with your mate. Such thoughtfulness shows your spouse that you do not take him or her for granted.

We rely on certain rituals and traditions to give us an opportunity to express our love for each other. We kiss each other goodnight and say, "May God bless your sleep." We celebrate our love on anniversaries and birthdays by giving each other small gifts. We telephone each other when we're apart, visit one of two favorite restaurants on special occasions, go out to lunch, attend the theater, and share hugs. All of these things—spontaneous little acts as well as carefully planned events—are ways to demonstrate that we love each other.

One word of caution: Be sure you are expressing your love in the language—the words and the actions—that your spouse will understand as love. Just because you feel loved when you plan a special dinner out doesn't mean that your spouse feels loved when you do the same for him! Be a student of your mate. Know what makes him "tick" and what makes him "ticked." Know what best communicates to each other the love you have. And keep your eyes open for common, everyday events that give you the chance to express that love!

Continually strive to make sure that your love is patient and kind and that it does not envy or boast and is not proud. It is a lifetime of challenge to develop a Christlike expression of love to each other.

Jerry and Barbara Cook offer another way to tell your mate that you love him.

I Need You

I need you in my times of strength and in my weakness;
I need you when you hurt as much as when I hurt.
There is no longer the choice as to what we will
    share:
We will either share all of life or be fractured persons.
I didn't marry you out of need or to be needed.
We were not driven by instincts or emptiness;
We made a choice to love.
But I think something supernatural happens at the
    point of marriage commitment (or maybe it's actu-
    ally natural).
A husband comes into existence; a wife is born.
He is a whole man before and after, but at a point in
    time he becomes a man who also is a husband;
That is—a man who needs his wife.
She is a whole woman before and after.
But from now on she needs him.
She is herself but now also part of a new unit.
Maybe this is what is meant in saying, "What God
    hath joined together."
Could it be He really does something special at "I do"?
Your despair is mine even if you don't tell me about it.
But when you do tell, the sharing is easier for me;
And you also can then share from my strength in that
weakness.[22]

Prayer

Father God, I want my wife to know that I love her. Teach me to be more open about my feelings. Help me be a student of my wife so that I know what actions and words make her feel loved. Amen.

Taking Action

- Do something for your wife that you hate doing but she loves—watching a romantic movie, going shopping when your favorite ball game is on TV.
- Send her flowers.
- Give her a certificate for a massage.
- Take care of the children while she goes on the church's women's retreat.
- Go out for coffee with your wife and talk about the day.

Reading On

1 Peter 4:7-11   1 John 4:7-21

There are moments in our lives so lovely that they transcend earth and anticipate heaven for us. This foretaste of eternity has made clear to me the perpetual and all-embracing service that friendship should ever be.

—*Helen Keller*

Teach Us to Number Our Days

Scripture Reading: Hebrews 9:11-28

Key Verse: Hebrews 9:27

> Man is destined to die once, and after that to
> face judgment.

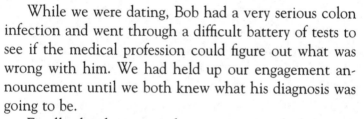

While we were dating, Bob had a very serious colon
infection and went through a difficult battery of tests to
see if the medical profession could figure out what was
wrong with him. We had held up our engagement announcement until we both knew what his diagnosis was
going to be.

Finally the day came when we were to find out just
how serious Bob's condition was. Naturally our thoughts
raced to the worst of conditions, and we thought maybe
the doctor was going to tell him he had only a year to
live. If so, what would our reactions be, and how would
we live out that year?

We didn't have to live out those concerns, because
the staff of doctors came back with a very positive report.
With some strong medication and an altered diet the infection cleared up, and within a few months Bob was
back to his regular routine. However, the basic question

"If I had just one year to live, what would I do?" is a good one for all of us to think through. What would we do?

A.W. Tozer wrote a response to this question. See if your thoughts might be similar to his.

> Suppose that I were to learn that I had just one year to live—the number of my days was to be only 365. What should I do with the precious few days that remained to me?
>
> The first thing is that I would have to arrive at some plan of action in conformity with known facts. I mean the facts of life and death and what God has to say about them in the Bible. However much I might ignore them while the hope of long life lay before me, with that hope shrunk to a brief year, these facts would take on tremendous proportions. With death stalking me, I would have little interest in trivial subjects and would instead be concerned with the essentials.
>
> I would stop hoping vaguely that somehow things would come out all right, and I would get down to realities. After all, the Bible says, "We are all as an unclean thing, and all our righteousnesses are as filthy rags" (Isaiah 64:6). And, "For whosoever shall keep the whole law, and yet offend in one point, he is guilty of all" (James 2:10). Knowing that "it is appointed unto men once to die, but after this the judgment" (Hebrews 9:27), I would take no rest until I had absolute assurance on these vital matters.

I would come to God on His own terms. It was Jesus who said, "I am the way, the truth, and the life; no man cometh unto the Father but by me" (John 14:6). I would not stand on ceremony nor allow myself to be hindered by the niceties of religion. For the Bible says, "Not by works of righteousness which we have done, but according to [God's] mercy he saved us" (Titus 3:5).

I would want to *know* that my sins were forgiven, that I had passed from death unto life, and that Jesus Christ was my personal Savior. "Neither is there salvation in any other; for there is no other name under heaven given among men whereby we must be saved" (Acts 4:12).

The Bible goes on to say, "Christ also hath once suffered for sins, the just for the unjust, that He might bring us to God" (1 Peter 3:18). He "was delivered [up to death] for our offenses, and was raised again for our justification" (Romans 4:25).

I would put away apathy, come boldly to Christ, and throw myself at His feet: "Believe on the Lord Jesus Christ, and thou shalt be saved." The Bible says, "For God so loved the world that he gave his only begotten Son, that whosoever believeth in him should not perish but have everlasting life" (Acts 16:31; John 3:16). I would come believing that God's promise of forgiveness and eternal life includes me.

Then, a new person in Christ, I would give the last remaining year to God. All the wreckage and loss of the years behind me would spur me on to make the one year before me a God-blessed success.

Now all this would seem to me to be the good and right thing to do for one who had just a year to live. But since we do not know whether we have a year before us, or a day or 10 days, and since what would be right for the last year would be right for the whole life—even if its years were many—then the conclusion is plain. Our cry to God should be, "Teach us to number our days, that we may apply our hearts to wisdom" (Psalm 90:12).

I do not know what others may want to do, but I want to get down to business and live as if this year were my last. Then, if God should spare me to a ripe old age, I can depart without regrets.

If *you* had just one year to live, what would *you* do?[23]

Prayer

Father God, teach us as a couple to number our days and to live each day, week, month, and year as if it were our last. May we reconfirm our purpose in life. Let us have the desire to live with Your purpose for our lives. Let us not waste time serving just ourselves. When we stand before You someday, we want you to say, "Well done, good and faithful servant." We want to be Your servants. Challenge us today in a new way.

Taking Action

- Write in your journals what you would do if you had just one year to live. Discuss these with your mate.

- In order to accomplish these ideas, what actions would need to take place? Begin to live out these plans. Check your calendar for next year to see how you've done.

- If you don't have a will or trust made out for you and your family, contact a reputable attorney and draw up these papers.

Reading On

- Read the various Scriptures given in today's study as given by A.W. Tozer.

Godly Wisdom in Discipline

Scripture Reading: Proverbs 3:11,12; 13:24; 15:13; 17:22; 22:15; 29:15.

Key Verse: Proverbs 15:13

> A happy heart makes the face cheerful, but heartache crushes the spirit.

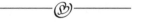

Parenting is an overwhelming task, and how to discipline our children is one of the most perplexing aspects of the job. Fortunately, as you saw in today's Scripture reading, the book of Proverbs contains some specific verses which offer good biblical principles for raising our children.

We often feel we are in a tug-of-war between child and parent. The natural tendency is to throw in the towel and give up. Far too often we have seen parents who have given up this task to gently yet firmly shape their child's will, as would a trainer of a wild animal or as the potter would a piece of clay. In his book *The Strong-Willed Child* James Dobson offers this insight:

> It is obvious that children are aware of the contest of wills between generations, and that is precisely

why the parental response is so important. When a child behaves in ways that are disrespectful or harmful to himself or others, his hidden purpose is often to verify the stability of the boundaries. This testing has much the same function as a policeman who turns doorknobs at places of business after dark. Though he tries to open doors, he hopes they are locked and secure. Likewise, a child who assaults the loving authority of his parents is greatly reassured when their leadership holds firm and confident. He finds his greatest security in a structured environment where the rights of other people (and his own) are protected by definite boundaries. [24]

It takes godly wisdom to provide this kind of security. How do we set and maintain stable boundaries? First, we must note that there is a difference between abuse and discipline. Proverbs 13:24 tells us that if we truly love our children, we will discipline them diligently. Abuse is unfair, extreme, and degrading. Such action doesn't grow out of love, but from hate. Abuse leads to a soiled self-image that often lasts a lifetime. Discipline, on the other hand, upholds the child's worth and is fair and fitting for the infraction.

Second, we must be sure the child understands the discipline he is to receive. When we disciplined Jenny and Brad, we spent a lot of time with them discussing what they did and making sure they understood what the infraction was. We realize that every child is different, so the way you approach each one will be through your knowledge of that particular child.

On occasion when a sterner approach was necessary,

we did give spankings. They were firmly applied to the beefy part of the buttocks, and they did hurt. Spankings were few and far between, though, and when they did occur, they were never given in anger. And afterward we talked again with the children about why they were disciplined and how they would behave differently in the future.

One of the main purposes of discipline in our home was to have the child realize that he or she is responsible for his actions and must be accountable for his or her behavior. Since every child is different, the methods of discipline will vary according to temperament. (In our day, we didn't have "Time Out." However, we've found this to be a very good technique, and we use it with our grandchildren very effectively.)

Whatever the type of discipline the infraction warranted, we always ended in prayer plus warm hugs and assuring words. This form of correction strengthens the child's spirit and helps him or her know the boundaries. Our love and concern for our kids and their well-being created stronger motivation for them to behave according to our family's conduct and behavior standards.

Third, when we discipline our children, we want to *shape* rather than *crush* our children's spirit. As Proverbs 15:13 teaches, you can look into the eyes of children around you to see those who are being crushed and those being shaped. Our goal as parents is to provide our children with solid direction and self-assurance that will see them throughout life. The child who is shaped with loving and firm discipline will have a love for life, but a crushed spirit produces a child with no hope for the future.

Fourth, our discipline must be balanced. We don't want to be so rigid that we don't allow our children to make mistakes, or so loose that family members are bouncing off the walls trying to find their boundaries. Children must know where the boundaries are and what the consequences are if they choose to go beyond these limits.

In Scripture we read about physical discipline. The writer of the Proverbs says, for instance, "Folly is bound up in the heart of a child, but the rod of discipline will drive it far from him" (Proverbs 22:15). Of course none of us wants to risk being an abusive parent, but hear what Dr. Dobson says about the importance of a child being able to associate wrongdoing with pain:

> If your child has ever bumped his arm against a hot stove, you can bet he'll never deliberately do that again. He does not become a more violent person because the stove burnt him; in fact, he learned a valuable lesson from the pain. Similarly, when he falls out of his high chair or smashes his finger in the door or is bitten by a grumpy dog, he learns about physical dangers in his world. These bumps and bruises throughout childhood are nature's way of teaching him what to fear. They do not damage his self-esteem. They do not make him vicious. They merely acquaint him with reality. In like manner, an appropriate spanking from a loving parent provides the same service. It tells him there are not only physical dangers to be avoided but he must steer clear of some social traps as well (selfishness, defiance, dishonesty, unprovoked aggression, etc.). [25]

Fifth, as you discipline your children, be consistent in your approach. Here are some guidelines:

- Make sure there is a clear understanding of the rules.
- Discipline in private. If you're in a public setting, wait until you can be alone.
- Review the infraction and its consequences.
- Be firm in your discipline.
- Assure your child of your love and concern.
- Hug your child after each disciplinary moment.
- End your session with a time of prayer. (Give your child an opportunity to pray too.)

As we look back over our child-rearing years, we realize we made plenty of mistakes. But when we did, we always tried to be the first to admit them to our children. So, even though you'll miss the mark occasionally, you will still be moving in a proper direction of discipline administered in love. Your children want to know their boundaries. Setting and enforcing clear boundaries is a gift of love to them that results in security and self-assurance they can carry through life.

Prayer

Father God, You know that we want for our children what is best for them. Give us the patience to get to know each of our children individually and then grant us the wisdom to know what kind of discipline will be most effective for each. Help us to be effective parents who train our children to love and serve You. Amen.

Taking Action

- Do you have a clear direction regarding the goal of your children's discipline? If not, spend some time today thinking about it and write down some of your ideas.

- Review these ideas with your mate.

- Tell each member in your family today that you love him or her, and give specific reasons why.

- Take a poll tonight at dinner. Ask each family member, "What's the best thing that happened to you today?" This will give you some insight into your children. (Parents must participate too.)

Reading On

Mark 12:28-31   1 Peter 5:5,6
Galatians 5:16   Colossians 3:17

How Did It Happen?

Scripture Reading: Galatians 5:7-10, 13-15

Key Verse: Galatians 5:7

> *You were running a good race. Who cut in on you and kept you from obeying the truth?*

———————⊗———————

The timer clicked, the TV screen fluttered, and the speaker blared the morning news.

"Morning already?" groaned Larry. He rolled over and squeezed the pillow tightly over his ears, not seriously thinking he could muffle the announcement of another day in the rat race. Then the aroma of coffee from the timer-operated percolator lured him toward the kitchen.

Six hours of sleep may not have been the house rule growing up, but success at the end of the twentieth century demanded a premium from its active participants. A rising star like Larry couldn't squander time sleeping.

Curls of steam rose from the bowl of instant oatmeal; the microwave had produced predictably perfect results in perfect cadence with his 35-minute wake-up schedule.

Slouched in his chair, propped against his elbow, Larry noticed the computer screen staring back at him. Last night he balanced his checkbook after the eleven o'clock news, and, weary from the long day, he must have neglected to switch it off.

His wife, Carol, had welcomed a day off, so she slept in. Larry went through the rote motions of getting the kids off to school. After the two younger children had been dropped off at daycare, he was alone in the car with Julie. Twelve-year-old Julie seemed troubled lately. "Daddy, do you love Mom anymore?" she asked. The question came out of the blue to Larry, but Julie had been building the courage to ask it for months. Their family life was changing, and Julie seemed to be the only member of the family diagnosing the changes. Larry reassured her he loved Mom very much.

Carol didn't plan to go back to work when she first started on her MBA degree. Bored with her traditional, nonworking-housewife role, she just wanted more personal self-fulfillment. Her magazines conferred no dignity on the role of mother-tutor.

Although her family satisfied her self-esteem need for many years, other neighborhood women her same age seemed to lead glamorous lives in the business world. She couldn't help but question her traditional values.

"Maybe I'm too old-fashioned—out of step with the times," she thought to herself.

So, two nights each week for three and a half years she journeyed off to the local university, a big investment—not to mention the homework. By the time she walked across the stage to receive her diploma, Carol was convinced women had a right to professional fulfillment just as much as men.

Larry, a tenacious, carefree sales representative, advanced quickly in his company. Fifteen years of dream chasing rewarded him with a vice-president's title. The pay covered the essentials, but they both wanted more of the good life.

"I've been thinking about going back to work," Carol told him.

Larry didn't protest. She had earned extra money as a bank teller at the beginning of their marriage, and the money helped furnish their honeymoon apartment. By mutual agreement, Carol stopped working when Julie was born, and ever since then they had been hardpressed to make ends meet.

Even though his own mother didn't work, Larry knew things were different for women. Still, he had mixed emotions about sending their two small children to a daycare center. But since money was always a problem, he just shrugged and kept silent when Carol announced she had started interviewing for a job.

Their neighbors bought a 24-foot cabin cruiser. Larry was surprised to learn they could own one too for only 328 dollars per month. By scrimping for five months they pulled together a thousand dollars, which, when added to their savings, gave them enough for the 2500-dollar down payment.

Larry loved cars. His gentle dad had always loved cars. If a shiny two-door pulled up to him at a traffic light, Larry's heart always beat faster—he could just picture himself shifting through the gears of a fancy European import. By accident he discovered that for only 423 dollars per month he could lease the car of his fantasies—a racy import! Leasing had never occurred to him before.

Carol desperately wanted to vacation in Hawaii that year; her Tuesday tennis partner went last spring. But they couldn't do both.

"If you go along with me on this one, I'll make it up to you, Carol. I promise!" Larry told her, his infectious grin spreading across his face. She reminisced how that impish, little-boy smile had first attracted her to him. He had been good to her, she thought.

"Okay, go ahead," Carol told him.

His dad had always loved Chevys. Larry's tastes had evolved with the times.

Carol dreamed of living in a two-story home with a swimming pool, but, with the car and boat payments so high, it remained a dream for years. Larry slaved 12- and 14-hour days, always thinking of ways to earn more money for Carol's dream house. When Carol went to work, they added up the numbers and were elated to see they could finally make the move.

The strain of keeping their household afloat discouraged them. There were bills to pay, kids to pick up from daycare, deadlines to meet, quotas to beat, but not much time to enjoy the possessions they had accumulated.

Words from a Simon and Garfunkel song haunted Larry's thoughts: "Like a rat in a maze, the path before me lies. And the pattern never alters, until the rat dies." He was trapped.

Carol pressured out—she just couldn't take it anymore. She believed Larry had let her down. He was supposed to be strong. He was supposed to know how to keep everything going. But Larry was just as confused about their situation as she was.

As the U-Haul van pulled away from the house Larry couldn't quite believe she was actually doing it—Carol was moving out. She said she just needed some time and space to sort things out, that she was confused. The question Julie had asked a few months earlier burned in his mind: "Daddy, do you love Mom anymore?" Yes . . . yes, he loved her, but was it too late? How did things get so out of hand?[26]

I'm sure you know your fair share of Larrys. In fact, Larry may even remind you of yourself. If so, let this be a wake-up call. No one wins the rat race! No one!

Are you trying to win the rat race? If so, you might consider making some dramatic changes before one of your children asks you, "Daddy, do you love Mommy?" and you find you can't honestly say yes.

Why do we run in a race that has no winners?

Prayer

Father God, we want to run this race called life for You. But it's hard for us to know how to get out of the rat race we feel so caught up in. Give us clarity. Help us to develop proper priorities—Your priorities for our lives and for our family. Help us to be the mate You want us to be. Give us couples who will point out our blind spots when they see them. We need to be accountable to another godly couple. Amen.

Taking Action

- Where do you see yourself in the story of Larry and Carol?

- How did you get caught up in the race that doesn't produce winners?

- What changes are you going to start making today?

- Have you ever wondered, "How did it happen?"

Reading On

1 Corinthians 6:12	Ecclesiastes 5:10
Romans 12:1,2	2 Corinthians 5:17

Bear Other's Burdens

Those who bear the Cross must also bear others' burdens. This includes the burden of responsibility for sin as well as the sharing of suffering. What room can there possibly be for touchiness or a self-regarding fastidiousness in the true burden-bearer? Forgiveness is a clear-eyed and coolheaded acceptance of the burden of responsibility.

—*Elisabeth Elliot*

You Are God's Unique Creation

Scripture Reading: Psalm 139:13-18

Key Verse: Psalm 139:14

> *I praise you because I am fearfully and wonderfully made; your works are wonderful, I know that full well.*

You're special. In all the world there's nobody like you.

Since the beginning of time there has never been another person quite like you.

Nobody has your smile, nobody has your eyes, your nose, your hair, your hands, your voice.

You're special. No one can be found who has your handwriting.

Nobody anywhere has exactly your tastes for food, clothing, music, or art.

No one sees things just as you do.

In all of time there's been no one who laughs like you, no one who cries like you; what makes you cry or laugh will never produce identical laughter and tears from anybody else, ever.

You're the only one in all of creation who has your particular set of abilities.

Oh, there will always be somebody who is better at one of the things you're good at, but no one in the universe can reach the quality of your combination of talents, ideas, abilities, and feelings. Like a room full of musical instruments, some may excel alone, but none can match the symphony sound when all are played together. You're a symphony.

Through all of eternity, no one will ever look, talk, walk, think, or do like you.

You're special . . . you're rare. And in all rarity there is great value. Because of your great value you need not attempt to imitate others; you will accept—yes, celebrate your differences.

You're special and you're beginning to realize it's no accident that you're special.

You're beginning to see that God made you special for a purpose.

He must have a job for you that no one else can do as well as you.

Out of the billions of applicants, only one is qualified, only one has the right combination of what it takes.

That one is you, because . . . you're special.[27]

Someone in your life—your spouse, your child—may need to hear these words today. And maybe that someone is you as a couple. Do you, like the psalmist, fully realize that you are "fearfully and wonderfully made"? Do your children and your spouse know that about themselves?

For a long time at our house we have reminded our children and ourselves that we are special with a red plate that reads "You Are Special." We use it for breakfasts, lunches, dinners, birthdays, anniversaries, and various other special occasions. We've used it at home, in restaurants, at

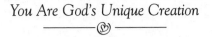
the park, and at the beach. Maybe that's a tradition you could start at your house.

You might also have every person at the meal tell the person being honored why that person is special to him or her. Give the person a chance to share why he thinks he or she is special.

Our red plate has become a very valuable tradition in our family. We all need to be reminded every once in a while that we truly are special.

Prayer

> *Father God, help me to realize that we are Your handiwork, "fearfully and wonderfully made," and therefore very special in Your sight. You knew us before we were made. You sent Your Son to die on the cross for our sins. Thank You for this amazing love, and help us to share it at home and let our family know how special they are to You and to us. Amen.*

Taking Action

- What are three things that make you unique?
- Who are you, the unique individual God fashioned? What makes you smile and laugh? What irritates you? What idiosyncrasies do you have?
- What helps you wind down?
- Now thank God for making you who you are.
- Write a note to a friend telling him or her why he is special to you.

Reading On

Psalm 40:5   Psalm 119:73

Shy, indecisive, and struggling people may welcome or even invite us to provide for them. They may even say "I can't" when they really mean "I don't want to put out whatever is needed." . . . And we average persons are . . . very vulnerable, in fact, to such manipulation. It is more immediately gratifying to say, "Of course I will do it for you" or to offer the advice, "What you really need to do is this. . . ." The right response in such cases usually provides much less immediate gratification. "Oh, come on, you can do it. . . . You have a good mind and you are capable of making decisions. What do you think you should do?" . . . What people really need is belief in themselves, confidence in their own ability to take on the problems and opportunities of life.

—*John Powell*

Develop a Plan for Your Life

Scripture Reading: Genesis 2:20b-25

Key Verse: Genesis 2:23

> *This is now bone of my bones and flesh of my flesh; she shall be called "woman," for she was taken out of man.*

———— ✍ ————

In his bestselling book *Talking Straight*, Lee Iacocca talks about the importance of the family:

> My father told me that the best way to teach is by example. He certainly showed me what it took to be a good person and a good citizen. As the old joke has it, "No one ever said on his deathbed, I should have spent more time on my business." Throughout my life, the bottom line I've worried about most was that my kids turn out all right.
>
> The only rock I know that stays steady, the only institution I know that works, is the family. I was brought up to believe in it—and I do. Because I think a civilized world can't remain civilized for long if its foundation is built on anything but the family. A city, state or country can't be any more

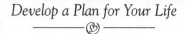
than the sum of its vital parts—millions of family units. You can't have a country or a city or a state that's worth . . . [anything] unless you govern within yourself in your day-to-day life.

It all starts at home."[28]

In our Scripture reading today we are reminded that God Himself established the family. Although today's secular world is trying its hardest to minimize the family as an institution, we know that whatever God begins He will not abandon in history.

The Bible is very clear in its teaching that woman was created for man and was to be his helper. Man and woman were designed for each other. That was God's plan. Do you have a plan for your family? Have you and your mate taken time to draft a master plan for your family? What is it to look like—what values, what guidelines, what aspirations?

Marriage causes a man to leave his mother and father and be united to his wife, becoming one flesh with her. Is this a description of what happened to you and your mate?

Scripture then states, "The man and his wife were both naked, and they felt no shame." One of our biggest challenges in life is to stand before each other naked, knowing that we aren't ashamed because we have followed God's plans for our family. Nakedness isn't always physical; it also includes emotional, spiritual, and psychological nakedness.

Furthermore, we must follow God's plans for having a healthy family if, as Mr. Iacocca points out, we are to survive as a society. It all starts at home, so let's make it our goal to follow God's plan. Take time to write down on paper what your plan for life is. Establish a theme verse that will help you prioritize the many pulls you have on your time, money, and services. You can't do it all. Establish and plan and follow the plan.

Prayer

> *Father God, create in us a hunger to search out Your plan for our lives and for our family. Give us the wisdom to major on the majors and not get sidetracked by the minors. It's easy to get distracted from Your plan, but we want to follow Your master plan for our lives. When life is over we want You to say, "Well done, good and faithful servant." Help us today. Amen.*

Taking Action

- Meet with your mate and begin to prayerfully design a master plan for your family.

- Write this plan down and include specific goals for each family member.

- Begin today to raise good children who know and want to serve the Lord.

Reading On

Genesis 18:19

What Is Life For?

You and I must open ourselves to the question: What is life for? We should get right down into the fabric of our daily lives. What am I doing? Is my life a series of deadlines . . . meetings . . . clearing my desk . . . answering phones . . . moving from one crisis to the next? Do I look forward to the stretch of life that is ahead of me? To next week? To the coming year? Is mine a hand-to-mouth existence? Is it a matter of "getting by"? . . . Am I in a survival context? Do I feel trapped? Am I just hanging on? Am I asking: How much longer can I take this?

—*John Powell*

They Will Become One

Scripture Reading: Genesis 2:20b-25

Key Verse: Genesis 2:24

> *For this reason a man will leave his father and mother and be united to his wife, and they will become one flesh.*

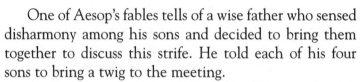

One of Aesop's fables tells of a wise father who sensed disharmony among his sons and decided to bring them together to discuss this strife. He told each of his four sons to bring a twig to the meeting.

As the young men assembled, the father took each boy's twig and easily snapped it in half. Then he gathered four twigs, tied them together in a bundle, and asked each son to try to break the bundle. Each one tried to no avail. The bundle would not snap.

After each son had tried valiantly to break the bundle, the father asked his boys what they had learned from the demonstration. The oldest son replied. "If we are individuals, anyone can break us, but if we stick together, no one can harm us." The father answered, "You are right. You must always stand together and be strong."

What is true for the four brothers is equally true for a

husband and wife. If we don't stand together and let God make us one in spite of our differences, we will easily be defeated. That is one reason why, in this passage, God calls a husband and wife to:

- *Departure* ("A man shall leave his father and his mother . . .")
- *Permanence* ("and shall cleave to his wife . . .")
- *Oneness* ("and they shall become one flesh")(NASB).

Together, these three elements help make a marriage strong. Let's first think about oneness.

In God's sight we become one at the altar when we say our vows to each another before Him. But practically speaking, oneness between a husband and wife is a process that happens over a period of time, over a lifetime together.

And becoming one with another person can be a very difficult process. It isn't easy to change from being independent and self-centered to sharing every aspect of your life and self with another person. The difficulty is often intensified when you're older and more set in your ways when you marry or, as was the case for Emilie and me, when the two partners come from very different family, religious, or financial background.

Emilie for instance, came from an alcoholic family and was raised by a verbally and physically abusive father. I came from a warm, loving family where yelling and screaming simply didn't happen. It took us only a few moments to say our vows and enter into oneness in God's eyes, but we have spent more than 38 years blending our lives and building the oneness which we enjoy today.

Becoming *one* doesn't mean becoming the *same*, however. Oneness means sharing the same degree of commitment to the Lord and to the marriage, the same goals and dreams, and the same mission in life. Oneness is internal conformity to one another, not an external conformity. It's not the Marines with their short haircuts, shiny shoes, straight backs, and characteristic walk. The oneness and internal conformity of a marriage relationship comes with the unselfish act of allowing God to shape us into the marriage partner He would have us be. Oneness results when two individuals reflect the same Christ. Such spiritual oneness produces tremendous strength and unity in a marriage and in the family.

For this oneness to happen, the two marriage partners must leave their families and let God make them one. Men help the cleaving happen when they *show*—not just *tell*—their wives that they are the most important priority after God. Likewise, our wife needs to let us know how important we are to her. Husbands cannot be competing with their wife's father or any other male for the number one position in her life. Men must know that their wife respects, honors, and loves them if they are to act out their proper role as a husband. And clear communication of their love for their wife will strengthen the bond of marriage and encourage her love and respect for him.

Now consider the words Paul wrote to the church at Philippi: "Make my joy complete by being of the same mind, maintaining the same love, united in spirit, intent on one purpose" (Philippians 2:2 NASB). This verse has guided us as we have worked to unite our family in purpose, thought, and deed. After many years of trial, error, and endless hours of searching, we can say that we are truly united in our purpose and direction. If you were to ask Emilie to state our purpose and direction, her answer would match mine: Matthew 6:33—"Seek first his kingdom and his righteousness, and all these things will be given to you." As we face decisions, we ask ourselves, "Are we seeking God's kingdom and His righteousness? Will doing this help His kingdom come and help us experience His righteousness? Or are we seeking our own edification or our own satisfaction?" These questions guide both of us whenever we have to decide an issue, and that oneness of purpose helps make our marriage work.

Larry Crabb points out another important dimension to the oneness of a husband and wife: "The goal of oneness can be almost frightening when we realize that God does not intend [only] that my wife and I find our personal needs met in marriage. He also wants our relationship to validate the claims of Christianity to a watching world as an example of the power of Christ's redeeming love to overcome the divisive effects of sin."[29]

God calls us to permanence and oneness in a marriage, qualities which the world neither values nor encourages. Knowing what God intends marriage to be—working to leave, cleave, and become one with our spouse—will help us shine God's light in a very dark world.

Prayer

> *Father God, today's reading has helped us realize that there are several areas in our lives where we need to be more united. Show us how to help work toward unity in purpose and spirit. We thank You now for what You are going to do in our marriage. Amen.*

Taking Action

- Set a date with your spouse and, when you're together, write down five things you agree on regarding family, discipline, manners, values, church, home, etc.

- At the same time, list any issues which you don't yet agree on. State the differences and discuss them. Agree to pray about these differences. Then set a time for another date to again discuss these items.

- Say "I love you" in a way you don't usually say it.
  —Fill a heart-shaped box with jelly beans, chocolates, or jewelry.
  —Give a certificate for a massage, a facial, or a weekend getaway.
  —Have firewood delivered—and then use it!

- Show your mate that you care when you pay attention to small details.
  —Instead of just handing him or her a pack of gum, unwrap a piece for him.
  —Place a flower on her pillow.
  —Offer to help with one of your mate's least-liked jobs.
  —Change clothes when you come home from the office.
  —Give your mate a compliment about her appearance.
  —Offer to pick up the children at childcare.
  —Drop by the cleaners and pick up the clothes.

Reading On

Philippians 2:2	Matthew 19:3-6
Matthew 6:33	1 Corinthians 6:19,20

What Is Your Entertainment and Information?

Scripture Reading: 1 Corinthians 6:12-20

Key Verse: 1 Corinthians 6:12

> *Everything is permissible for me—but not everything is beneficial.*

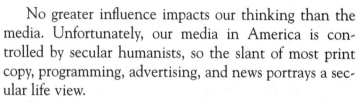

No greater influence impacts our thinking than the media. Unfortunately, our media in America is controlled by secular humanists, so the slant of most print copy, programming, advertising, and news portrays a secular life view.

Secular humanism is the view that man establishes his own moral values apart from the influence of anyone (including God), and he self-determines his own destiny; he is the "master of his own fate."

The problem with such a life view is that it has no absolutes, but everything is relative; it has no eternal reference point. We can make up our own rules as we go. But how do we know if sexual promiscuity is immoral or not? Why shouldn't we cheat in business? Why should family life be valued higher than career?

Ted Koppel, the news anchor for ABC's Nightline, in a 1987 commencement address at Duke University said:

"We have reconstructed the Tower of Babel and it is a television antenna, a thousand voices producing a daily parody of democracy in which everyone's opinion is afforded equal weight regardless of substance or merit. Indeed, it can even be argued that opinions of real weight tend to sink with barely a trace in television's ocean of banalities." This relativistic approach means we need to guard our minds more carefully, because so many kooky ideas are floating around.

Through the media and advertising, which rely heavily on subliminal suggestions, we are consciously and unconsciously lured to go for the Madison Avenue lifestyle. The secret of fanning our smoldering desires and wants has been elevated to a scientific approach. The economic goal of television is, after all, to sell products and services!

Our problem may be more what our *unconscious* minds are exposed to than our conscious minds. According to Wilson Bryan Key in his book *Subliminal Seduction:*

> The conscious mind discriminates, decides, evaluates, resists or accepts. The unconscious, apparently, merely stores units of information, much of which influences attitudes or behavior at the conscious level in ways about which science knows virtually nothing. The vast communication industry realized long ago the resistance to advertising which develops at the conscious level. However, there is little if any resistance encountered at the unconscious level, to which marketing appeals as now directed.

You see, we can at least somewhat defend ourselves at the conscious level, but most of consumerism's appeals are directed to our unconscious mind.

Perhaps the only way to overcome this dilemma is to reevaluate our sources of entertainment and information. Personally, we have virtually stopped watching television and are trying to read more books. First Corinthians 6:12 offers us a credo worth adopting:

"Everything is permissible for me"—but not everything is beneficial. "Everything is permissible for me"—but I will not be mastered by anything.

Our concern is that our unconscious mind would be mastered in an area in which we have no ability to resist. Our unconscious mind has no walls around it and no sentinel at the gate.

Watch television commercials one evening and ask yourself, "If these commercials are true, then who am I and what am I?" The life portrayed on the tube loves pleasure and sensuality, doesn't deny itself anything, and has a right to whatever goal it sets. I believe you will come to the same conclusion I did.

Recently Oldsmobile introduced an all-new Cutlass: new body style, reduced size, front-wheel drive. But the car met with very sluggish sales performance. We have a theory which the general manager of a local dealership concurs with: Since the changes in the car are so radical, people are waiting to buy them until they understand "who" and "what" they are if they own one.

In other words, because much of our identity is tied to what kind of car we drive, an advertising campaign is needed to define who and what we are if we drive this new Cutlass. Since it is a well-built, stylish car, sales will surely take off like a rocket as soon as the car is positioned properly. That's the power of the media.

Remember the heroes you grew up with? Roy Rogers, Gene Autry, Sky King, John Wayne—men of adventure, honor, and justice. The prime-time heroes of our contemporary society are shaped by the creative penmanship of morally bankrupt humanists. Frankly, we believe they represent a minority view.

Many great examples of genuine accomplishment, faith, and courage abound, but they are supplanted by the neutered characters of the media owners.

Wouldn't we all want the models for our children to be in the sacrifices and contributions of famous scientists, artists, thinkers, missionaries, statesmen, builders, and other heroes and saints? They are out there, but we are not going to find them through the media.[30]

Patrick Morley gives us a lot to think about in this excerpt from his book *The Man in the Mirror.* The insidious power of television is destroying our family life. As parents we have to take control of what we allow to come into our homes. We would call the police if a burglar entered our homes and stole something of value—but that is exactly what television is doing. As our key verse today teaches, what is permissible is not always beneficial. This is a warning to heed when we're considering the power of TV.

Think about the role that TV plays in your home. Are you or your family members addicted to television? Can you go a week without having the television on? Try it and see what happens. If nerves are on edge, tempers are flaring, and people are angry, these could be signs that you're too dependent on television for entertainment and escape. As a father, take the lead in getting this stealer of time under control. Be very selective in what comes in and when. Block out TV during those times when the family comes together for meals, discussion, activities, and homework.

Prayer

> *Father God, You know that we want the best for our family. We want to protect them from all that would hurt and rob them. Make us aware of those things which steal from us. Give us the courage to be strong in this and, if necessary, to turn off the television in our home. Amen.*

Taking Action

- Evaluate the amount of time that you and/or your family watch television. What kinds of programs do you watch? If they are sending false messages about life, you may want to develop an alternate plan for using your time more efficiently.

- What could you and your family do instead of watching television? Here are some ideas: Go to a play or a concert; have a picnic; watch family slides/movies; read books; listen to good music; talk together about life, the day-to-day and the big picture; take a walk; exercise; jog; swim; etc. Choose one to do this weekend and a second to do next weekend.

- What can you do to build up the family when so much of society is trying to tear it down? What activities can you plan?

Reading On

Ephesians 4:29
1 Corinthians 10:23, 24

Ten Rules that Work

Scripture Reading: Exodus 20:1-17

Key Verse: Exodus 20:8

> *Remember the Sabbath day by keeping it holy.*

———————— ✿ ————————

In looking at great successes we find certain strands that weave through a family, a career, a marriage, a church, or any kind of organization that rises above the commonness we see in everyday life. Sam Walton of Wal-Mart is a household word. One of the most recognizable names in the history of American business.

One thing you'll notice if you spend very much time talking with Sam about WalMart's success. He's always saying things like "This was the key to the whole thing," or "That was our real secret." He knows as well as anyone that there wasn't any magic formula. A lot of different things made it work, and in one day's time he may cite all of them as the "key" or the "secret." What's amazing is that for almost fifty years he's managed to focus on all of them at once—all the time. That's his real secret.[31]

—David Glass

In Sam's autobiography he gives ten principles that worked for his business. As we look at these, we can transfer the concepts to our marriages.

1. *Commit to your business.* Believe in it more than anyone else. Create a passion for it.
2. *Share your profits.* Treat all members of the company as partners. Behave as a servant leader in the partnership.
3. *Motivate your partners.* Each day think of new and more interesting ways to motivate and challenge your partners.
4. *Communicate everything you possibly can to your partner.* The more they know, the more they will understand.
5. *Appreciate everything your associates do for the business.* Nothing else can quite substitute for a few well-chosen, well-timed sincere words of praise.
6. *Celebrate your successes.* Don't take yourself too seriously, loosen up, have fun, laugh often, and show enthusiasm often.
7. *Listen to everyone in your company.* Figure out ways to get the partners talking. Listen when they do talk.
8. *Exceed your customer's expectations.* Stand behind everything you do. Customers will come back when they are valued.
9. *Control your expenses better than your competition.* You can make a lot of different mistakes and still recover if you run an efficient operation.
10. *Swim upstream.* Go the other way. Ignore the conventional wisdom. You can find your niche by going in exactly the opposite direction.

As God gave Moses the Ten Commandments, which have guided civilized man throughout history, he has also given good business people basic principles which help structure the workings of a successful business. All of these principles are useful in establishing basic guidelines for our lives as Christians—in business and in our family units. Develop a plan and begin to purposely live out that plan. Don't drift through life looking for direction; it can easily be found. You have to take hold of it and make it part of your life.

Prayer

Father God, let us take both sets of today's principles and make them part of our lives. We recognize that we have spiritual needs that require Your laws, and that our businesses and family life needs them. The other principles, inspired by You and developed by honorable men and women in business, will help our business and family life also. Help us to integrate both sets into our everyday life. Amen.

Taking Action

- Review the ten principles by Sam Walton, and see how they can apply to a successful marriage and family life.

- In your journal, jot down each principle and list at least three activities you could do to practice that principle which would strengthen your marriage and family unit.

- On a 3" x 5" card write down these ten words: Commit

Share
Motivate
Communicate
Appreciate
Celebrate
Listen
Exceed
Control
Swim

Carry the card with you, post it on a bulletin board, attach it to your sun visor in your car, adhere it to your refrigerator—anywhere that will make you consciously review these basic principles.

Reading On

Exodus 23:12   Leviticus 26:2
Exodus 31:13-16   Deuteronomy 6:6-9

Your Mate As
A Friend

Scripture Reading: Philippians 2:1-11
Key Verse: Philippians 2:2

> *Then make my joy complete by being like-minded, having the same love, being one in spirit and purpose.*

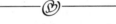

In my hometown an obscure nurseryman died recently. His name was Hubert Bales, and he was the shyest man I ever met. When he talked, he squirmed, blinked his eyes rapidly, and smiled nervously.

Hubert never ran in influential circles. He grew shrubs and trees, working with his hands the plot of land left him by his father. He was anything but an extrovert.

Yet when Hubert died, his funeral was the largest in the history of our little town. There were so many people that they filled even the balcony of the church.

Why did such a shy man win the hearts of so many people? Simply because, for all his shyness, Hubert knew how to make friends. He had mastered the principles of caring, and for more than 60 years he had put people first. Perhaps because they recognized that his generosity of spirit was an extra effort for someone so retiring, people loved him back. By the hundreds.[32]

Friendship is the launching pad for every love. It spills into the other important relationships of life. Friendship is the beginning of all levels of intimacy—with our mate, with our parents, with our children—with everyone we encounter.

Few of us are privileged to be able to sit down and share our most innermost thoughts with someone. Our society lets women be more intimate with each other than the man-to-man relationships. Girls can walk to school holding hands, shed an occasional tear, and say openly, "You are my best friend and I love you." It's hard for boys to be that close, though, because our culture says that it's not acceptable, normal behavior for them.

Women, that's why you might have to share often with your husband how to be soft and tender. He may have never had a proper model to show how to be a close friend and lover.

Research points out that friendly people live longer than the general population. Jesus thought that love and friendship were so important, He gave a new commandment in John 13:34,35:

> Love one another. As I have loved you, so you must love one another. By this all men will know that you are my disciples, if you love one another.

"But how do I develop friends?" you ask. We have found the following basic principles in the development of all friendships:

- Make friendships a top priority
- Be willing to take a risk, and be transparent
- Talk about your love for each other
- Learn and exhibit the language of love
- Give your friends room to be themselves

Unlike most popular thought, you don't have to be an outgoing extrovert to have friends. Like Hubert, in our opening story, you can be quiet, reserved, introverted, and still have many friends. If you care for people, you will have many friends. Begin caring for yourself, then branch out to your mate, children, parents, church, neighbors, club members, and other people.

Prayer

Father God, may we truly learn to care for others. First teach us to love You. We know we can't love others, if we don't love You first, ourselves second, and others third. Help us to care for ouselves and the people in our lives. We sometimes get so upset because we don't do what we know we should do. When we're mad at ourselves, we have a tough time loving others. I truly want to make my mate my special friend. Help me have a new beginning today. Amen.

Taking Action

- List in your journal how you rate your friendship factor: poor, marginal, good.

- In your journal, list the things you do to show you care for your spouse. Also list areas that need to be improved.

- Write two activities beside each deficiency that will help strengthen you in those areas.

- Discuss with your mate those areas in which you want to improve. Ask him or her to help you be accountable. Check in every few days to see how you are doing.

Reading On

Ephesians 5:21   Proverbs 18:24
Proverbs 17:17   John 15:13

Together Is Better

Scripture Reading: Matthew 19:1-12

Key Verse: Matthew 19:5

> *For this reason a man will leave his father and mother and be united to his wife, and the two will become one flesh.*

———— ⟲ ————

Wildlife biologists tell us that a flock of geese, by flying in a "V" formation, actually add at least 71 percent more flying range than if each bird was flying on its own. As each bird flaps its wings, it creates an updraft for the bird immediately following it. Left to itself, the lone goose experiences drag and resistance that causes it to tire quickly. When the lead bird in the formation tires, it simply rotates back in the wing and another goose flies the point.

Draft horses experience a similar, if earthbound, dynamic. Draft horses were made for pulling. Some years ago at a midwestern county fair, the champion animal pulled a sled weighing 4,500 pounds. The second-place animal dragged 4,000 pounds. Then someone proposed harnessing the two big fellas together, to see what they could do as a team. Together, they pulled 12,000 pounds![33]

Shouldn't we, as married couples with families grasp this basic principle of life: Two are better than one?

Scripture teaches us to be of:

- one mind
- one body
- one flesh
- one spirit
- one love
- one church

- one purpose
- one hope
- one Lord
- one God
- one mediator
- one, one, one . . .

Yet we try to go it alone. This loneness will be our destruction; man and woman were not made to be alone. We must rely upon each other's strengths to cover our weaknesses.

When Emilie and I were dating, I readily recognized that she was much stronger in some areas of life than I was. I also recognized quickly that if we combined her strengths and my strengths, we each would be stronger than if we went our separate ways.

To be one in marriage, a couple must be strong in the Lord. When we are one in Him, Satan cannot break us."

Prayer

> *Father God, at times we catch ourselves going our own separate ways. We forget that we are a team, and that our strength is in our togetherness. Thank You for reminding us today that each of us has strengths that need to be used in our home, family, and marriage. Thank You for giving me a mate who wants to work as a team. I truly need my mate to make me complete. Amen.*

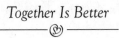
Taking Action

- List in your journal your mate's strengths. Put an X by those traits that you appreciate and that help make your marriage strong.

- Discuss and encourage your mate to use those strengths that aren't being used as much in your marriage.

- As a couple, discuss areas of weaknesses that need to be strengthened in order to become a better unit. Take the risk and be transparent in these areas.

Reading On

Matthew 19:5   Ephesians 4:4
John 10:30

I Will Bless
the Lord

Scripture: Psalm 34:1-7

Key Verse: Psalm 34:1

> *I will extol [bless] the LORD at all times; his praise will always be on my lips.*

———————— ✍ ————————

On November 8, 1994, Scott and Janet Willis and six of their children were traveling on Interstate Highway 94 when a bracket fell from a truck and punctured their mini-van's gas tank, causing a fire and explosion that instantly claimed the lives of five of their children, and the eventual death of a sixth child. Janet and Scott escaped only because they were sitting in the front of the van where the flames had not yet engulfed them.

As the story circled the media, anyone listening to their faith in God, their intense love for their children, and their grace-filled compassion towards the truck driver, had to be moved by this extraordinary couple. As I prayed for their situation, I kept remembering Janet's gentle peaceful face. Sit down with us as this humble woman shares some of her thoughts.

"The children and I were sleeping in the van when the accident occurred. Scott told me to get out of the car. In order to do that I had to dip my hands into a roaring fire to unlatch my safety belt. I then fell out the door while the car was still moving. Everything was wild! I ended up on the side of the road on my knees screaming, 'No God, not my children, no, no, no!' Scott got to me and said, 'It was quick. They are with the Lord. Janet this is what we have been prepared for.'

I realized I had been saying, 'no, no, no,' to God as my children were entering heaven's doors. I was saying, 'no God' to the very thing I ultimately wanted most for our children—to be with God eternally. I forced myself to repeat Psalm 34. 'I will bless the Lord at all times.'"

God had been preparing them for this time. All of the lessons, all of the preparation of the promises, all of the spiritual fiber He had woven into them has held Scott and Janet Willis together.

Janet said, "We have thrown ourselves into God's grace."[34]

Wow! What an extraordinary example of one couple living out the gospel. They truly have captured the whole essence of the Christian life. They understand why we are placed upon this earth. As Paul knew when he wrote to the church at Corinth, "My grace is sufficient for you, for my power is made perfect in weakness. . . . For when I am weak, then I am strong" (2 Corinthians 12:9,10).

Oh, if we in the church today could only grasp the concept that Christ's grace is sufficient and it's all that we need! There is great peace in acknowledging and accepting the sufficiency of God's grace by allowing Him to be strong during our periods of weaknesses. As human beings, we want to be strong and not allow Him to be strong for us. But He is all we need.

Prayer

> *Father God, Oh, how my heart aches for this family who has lost so much. I can't even begin to imagine the pain associated with such a tragedy. Thank You for giving us a model that reflects a powerful understanding of Your grace. May we as a couple grasp Your sufficiency in our lives. During our weaknesses, may we come to depend upon Your power and strength more and more, and not our own. Thank You for being there when we need You. Amen.*

Taking Action

- Thank God for the health and safety of your family.

- Tell each member of your family that you love them. Take time to write a note expressing your love for them.

- As a couple, discuss how you would be able to endure a similar tragedy in your life. Is God's grace sufficient for you?

Reading On

Romans 8:28   James 4:6
1 Corinthians 1:25-31   2 Corinthians 12:9-10
Romans 16:20

I Have a Delightful Inheritance

Scripture Reading: Psalm 16:1-11

Key Verse: Psalm 16:6

> *The boundary lines have fallen for me in pleasant places; surely I have a delightful inheritance.*

"Most heirs want only the money, not family heirlooms, treasures, or Bibles. The past means nothing to them, nor the future. However much education they have, they are barbarians. The modern barbarian may be a university graduate, a scientist, an artist, a person of prominence and wealth, but he is someone with no respect for the past, nor roots in it, nor any concern for the future. If he receives an inheritance, he wants to liquidate it, to turn it into cash. Rootless people live rootless lives."[35]

I guess one of the reasons we love our farm barn home is because it identifies with the fond memories of the past. We get to relive the hard work and sweat that went on before us. Our barn home also lets us decorate with some of the timeless antiques of bygone years. The rustic feel of the woods, windows, doors and the old sycamore, elm, and ash trees bring cooling on hot days of summer; we experience the coolness of the past.

Stub Weber in his new book, *Locking Arms*, states:

> Heritage matters. People need clear, steady tracks to follow. It's by divine design. We're linked to people who've walked the long path before us. We're linked to those who tread the trail behind. Not so very long ago, God himself left clear human footprints in the dust of our little world, tracks infinitely more indelible than those left by Apollo astronauts on the airless moon. Memory is the great encourager of spirit and life, of connectedness. And rehearsing the past is a sacred practice. It sets the present course. It gives perspective.[36]

Last year we had the pleasure to be in Abilene, Texas, doing a seminar. We took an extra day to drive to Bob's birthplace in Hawley, and then continued on to his grandfather's homestead in Anson. We drove out to the farm for the first time in forty-five years. As we drew near, I could see countless memories flash before Bob's eyes. He quickly went back in time to share the memories of the past. The buildings had long been torn down, but he escorted me to the site of the home, the cellar, the barn, and the pastures where the horses roamed. For the first time, I was able to actually see what my husband had shared with me during our married life. We took pictures to recapture the fondness of the past, and Bob even brought home an old brick from the foundation.

In this age, when families move and roots aren't able to go deep, we need to take the time to share with our family elements of our inheritance. What has gone before us is very important to who we are today. Our grandchildren love to sit in our laps, and go through picture albums that have been maintained over the years. "This was great grandad, this is Aunt Maria, this is Cousin Terri." Each of our grandchildren have their own albums from the day Mom went to the hospital pregnant and came home with a precious child of God. They beg us to tell them stories over and over of when they were babies.

Are you building a delightful inheritance for your children? Will they look back and say they had rich experiences growing up? Do they know who they are? Can they recognize the pillars of your families? If not, we encourage you to pass on timeless treasures so they can know from whence they came.

As David concludes Psalm 16: "You have made known to me the path of life; you will fill me with joy in your presence, with eternal pleasures at your right hand" verse 11.

Does your family major in the majors and minor in the minors? As your time comes to be with God in heaven, have you left strong, deep tracks for those left behind to follow? If not, start today. Begin to live with a purpose.

Prayer

Father God, Thank You for giving me a delightful inheritance—one that has been easy to follow because the tracks made by Your followers were so clear and leading in the right direction.

Were they perfect? No, but they had a consistency that lead me to You. I know there are those who have troubled pasts. They don't want to follow the tracks that were planted before them. Please give these people the courage and abundance of faith in You to have a new beginning. I thank You for Your Word which lights my path. Thank You for all You've done in the past, all that You are continuing to do in my life. Amen.

Taking Action

- In your journal, enter specifics about your delightful inheritance.

- Write down some great memories you have of grandfather, grandmother, an aunt or uncle, who impacted your life.

- Tonight at the dinner table, go around and have each member of the family share some exciting moments of the past.

- Start a photo album of each member of the family, if you haven't already done so.

Reading On

John 3:16   Malachi 2:5

Biblical Promises for Couples

- My dear brothers, take note of this: Every one should be quick to listen, slow to speak, and slow to become angry, for man's anger does not bring about the righteous life that God desires.

  —James 1:19,20

- Whoever believes in the Son has eternal life, but whoever rejects the Son will not see life, for God's wrath remains on him.

  —John 3:36

- Give, and it will be given to you. A good measure, pressed down, shaken together and running over, will be poured into your lap. For with the measure you use, it will be measured to you.

  —Luke 6:38

- All your sons will be taught by the Lord, and great will be your children's peace.

  —Isaiah 54:13

- The Lord is my rock, my fortress and my deliverer; my God is my rock, in whom I take refuge. He is my shield and the horn of my salvation, my stronghold.

  —Psalm 18:2

- Keep your lives free from the love of money and be content with what you have, because God has said, "Never will I leave you; never will I forsake you."

  —Hebrews 13:5

- The Lord disciplines those He loves, as a father the son he delights in.

  —Proverbs 3:12

- Wait for the Lord; be strong and take heart and wait for the Lord.

  —Psalm 27:14

- He gives strength to the weary and increases the power of the weak.

  —Isaiah 40:29

- Even though I walk through the valley of the shadow of death, I will fear no evil, for you are with me; your rod and your staff, they comfort me.

  —Psalm 23:4

- The Lord your God is the one who goes with you to fight for you against your enemies to give you victory.

  —Deuteronomy 20:4

- I write these things to you who believe in the name of the Son of God so that you may know that you have eternal life.

  —1 John 5:13

- It is by grace you have been saved, through faith—and this not from yourselves, it is the gift of God.

  —Ephesians 2:8

- God did not give us a spirit of timidity, but a spirit of power, of love and of self-discipline.

  —2 Timothy 1:7

- This is my prayer: that your love may abound more and more in knowledge and depth of insight.

  —Philippians 1:9

"I'm Too Busy Sawing"

Scripture Reading: Exodus 20:8,11

Key Verses: Exodus 20:9,10

> *Six days you shall labor and do all your work,*
> *but the seventh day is a Sabbath to the Lord*
> *your God. On it you shall not do any work.*

———————— ✍ ————————

In *The Seven Habits of Highly Effective People*, author Steven R. Covey tells a story that reflects the need for rest, renewal, and reawakening in our lives.

Suppose you come upon a man in the woods feverishly sawing down a tree.

"You look exhausted!" you exclaim. "How long have you been at it?"

"Over five hours," he replies, "and I'm beat. This is hard."

"Maybe you could take a break for a few minutes and sharpen that saw. Then the work would go faster."

"No time," the man says emphatically. "I'm too busy sawing."

To sharpen the saw means renewing ourselves in all four aspects of our natures:

Physical—exercise, nutrition, stress management;

Mental—reading, thinking, planning, writing;

Social/Emotional—service, empathy, security;

Spiritual—spiritual reading, study, and meditation.

To exercise in all these necessary dimensions,
we must be proactive. No one can do it for us
or make it urgent for us. We must do it for
ourselves.[37]

Can you identify with that man in the woods? We
can. We know how hard it is to stop sawing even though
we know that taking a break will help us come back to
our tasks stronger. And you may be a lot like us. But
we've learned to take some breaks—and you can, too.

In the "Taking Action" section, you'll find some ideas
for what to do when you stop sawing—and some of them
may sound so good that they'll help you put the saw
down. When you do—when you take time to renew yourself—you'll be better equipped to handle the demands
and stresses of life.

Like all of His commands, God's command to keep
the Sabbath—to take time for rest—is for your own good.
If you're tired and weary and maybe even fearful of what
will happen if you put down the saw, if you're uptight,
tense, and short-tempered, you are ready for renewal and
reawakening. Take the risk and see what happens.

Prayer

*Father God, we're often overwhelmed by all
that needs to be done. It often feels that we just*

don't have time to stop sawing. Living a balanced life seems like an unreachable goal. Help us. Teach us moderation. Show new balance. Amen.

Taking Action

- Below you'll find a variety of suggestions for things you can do to find refreshment. So take a risk. Stop sawing and see what it's like to live a life that's more in balance.

Physical

- Get a professional massage or take a sauna or steam bath.
- Exercise regularly by walking, jogging, playing racquetball, swimming, etc.
- Read a book on nutrition and begin to change your eating habits.
- Take a stress management class.
- Take a walk on the beach, by the lake, or along a mountain trail.
- Plant a garden.
- Walk or run in the rain.
- Volunteer for the United Way, the Cancer Society, or the Heart Association.
- Help a friend in need.

Mental

- Listen to good music.
- Read a good magazine or book.

- Find a spot for meditating and reflecting.
- Spend some time alone.
- Write a letter to an old friend.
- Write out some goals for the next three months.
- Enroll in a class at a local college.
- Think of possible changes in your life.
- List everything for which you are thankful.
- Learn to play an instrument.
- Memorize a favorite passage of Scripture.

Social/Emotional

- Have a good cry (yes, you men can cry too).
- Have breakfast or lunch with a friend.
- Spend a day doing anything you want.
- Spend a quiet weekend together just to regroup. Choose someplace close. Avoid a long drive.
- Visit a friend.
- Make a new friend.
- Volunteer your time at a school, hospital, or church.
- Help a friend in need.

Spiritual

- Read the Psalms.
- Meditate on Scripture. Read a short passage and think long and hard about it.

- Read a book by a Christian writer.

- Join a couples' Bible study.

- Visit someone at the hospital or nursing home.

- Examine your motives (are you self-serving or serving others?).

- Listen to good inspirational music.

- Now add your own ideas to each of the four lists. Learn to take a break and take care of yourself. God Himself knows the importance of rest. He gave us the Sabbath and He calls us to be good stewards of the body, mind, and spirit He gave us. It's more than okay to take care of yourself—it's essential!

Reading On

Matthew 22:36-40   Exodus 20:2-18

Do not think that love, in order to be genuine, has to be extraordinary. What we need is to love without getting tired. . . . Be faithful in small things because it is in them that your strength lies.

—Mother Teresa

The Minimum Daily Adult Requirement

Scripture Reading: Ephesians 2:4-9
Key Verses: Ephesians 2:8,9

> For it is by grace you have been saved, through faith—and this not from yourselves, it is the gift of God—not by works, so that no one can boast.

Several years ago a young college student asked, "As a Christian, how much beer can I drink?" Others have asked:

- How long should I read my Bible each day?
- How long should I pray each day?
- How much money do I have to give to the church?
- Do I have to sing in the choir to be a good Christian?
- How many times a week must I be in church?
- Do I have to _____, _____, _____?

The list goes on and on. We all want to know what the minimum daily adult requirement is for being a Christian. What do we really have to do, day-by-day, to get by?

We're interested in daily nutritional requirements

when it comes to our food. Shouldn't we be as concerned when it comes to our Christian walk and our spiritual health? Of course! It only makes sense that we would want to know how long Christians should pray, how long we should read the Bible, how much money we should put in the offering plate, how many church activities we should participate in each week, etc., etc.!

Paul addresses these very basic concerns in his letter to the Ephesians. He very clearly states, "For it is by grace you have been saved, through faith—and this not from yourselves, it is the gift of God—not by works, so that no one can boast" (verses 8,9). Said differently, Christ has freed us from bondage to minimum daily adult requirements. Our relationship with the Lord Jesus is not contingent on works; it is a gift of grace.

"So," you ask, "do I do nothing as a Christian? Aren't there any requirements?" The Scriptures challenge us to be like Christ, and if we are to do that, we need to open the Bible and learn how Jesus lived. When we do so, we see that Jesus

- Studied God's Word
- Spent time with believers
- Prayed regularly
- Served those around Him who were in need

Christ did not do these things because He was told to do them. He did them because He wanted to do them. He did them out of love.

So what is your minimum daily adult requirement when it comes to your spiritual health? It will be determined by love. So let your loving God guide you as you go through your day and let your love for Him shape your Bible study, prayer time, giving, and other church involvement. Your walk will look different from everyone else's. That's okay when you're sure you're doing what God wants you to do.

Prayer

> *Father God, help us not to worry about "how long" or "how often" as we try to live a life that pleases You. Put a strong desire in our souls to spend time with You today in prayer and study not so that we are doing what we "should," but because we love You and want to know You better. And in those quiet moments, let time stand still and help us forget about our schedules, commitments, and pressures as we worship You. Amen.*

Taking Action

- List the things you are doing because you "should," because you think they are required of you as Christians. Cross off those items you are doing joylessly out of a sense of compulsion.

- Why are you still doing those things left on your list? Cross out any other items which you are doing because you "should" rather than because you love God.

- Now list only those activities you want to do because you love the Lord and want to be more like Christ. You may not change your lists with this instruction, but now the items are listed because you want to do them rather than because you feel you should. Simply stated, you are learning to live out of grace, not the law.

Reading On

1 Corinthians 1:4-8   Ephesians 6:10
2 Timothy 1:9,10   James 4:6
2 Corinthians12:9

Harmony in the Home

Scripture Reading: Ephesians 3:14-21

Key Verses: Ephesians 3:17-19

> *I pray that you, being rooted and established
> in love, may have power, together with all the
> saints, to grasp how wide and long and high
> and deep is the love of Christ, and to know
> this love that surpasses knowledge—that you
> may be filled to the measure of all the fullness
> of God.*

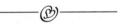

A traveler in Germany saw an unusual sight in the tavern where he stopped for dinner. After the meal, the landlord put a great dish of soup on the floor and gave a loud whistle. Into the room came a big dog, a large cat, an old raven, and a very large rat with a bell about its neck. All four went to the dish and, without disturbing each other, ate together. After they had eaten, the dog, the cat, and the rat lay before the fire, while the raven hopped around the room. These animals had been well trained by the landlord. Not one of them tried to hurt any of the others. The traveler's comment was, if a dog, a rat, a cat, and a bird can learn to live happily together, little children—even brothers and sisters—ought to be able to do the same.

Sadly, however, families are too often characterized by disharmony. When that's the case, we do well to model our prayers for our family after Paul's words in today's reading. The things he prays for can lead to harmony at home.

- Pray that your family may be "rooted and established in love" (verse 17). God's love can help us be patient and kind with one another. God's love is not envious, boastful, or proud. His love is not rude, self-seeking, or easily angered, and it does not keep track of wrongs. Furthermore, it protects, trusts, hopes, and perseveres (see 1 Corinthians 13:4-7). Isn't this the kind of love you want in your family? Then ask God to fill your home and your hearts with His love.

- Pray that each member of your family would be able "to grasp how wide and long and high and deep is the love of Christ" for him or her (verse 18). Knowing Christ's immeasurable love for us, knowing that He loves us just as we are, knowing that He made us special and unique, and knowing that He died for our sins enables us to love one another. May the members of your family begin to grasp the vastness of Christ's love for them, individually and collectively, so that they can more freely love each other.

- Pray that each family member would "know this love that surpasses knowledge" (verse 19). Because of our human limitations, such as they are, we can not fully comprehend God's love for us, a love that let Jesus die for us. God's love is beyond our knowledge of human love. But accepting in faith this gracious love helps us live out the gospel in our life and in our family.

- Pray that each member of your family will "be filled to the measure of all the fullness of God" (verse 19). Each day we read God's Word, we learn more about His patience, mercy, forgiveness, joy, justice, kindness, compassion—the list goes on and on. Can you imagine being filled completely full with these characteristics of God? Can you imagine each member of your family being filled with these qualities? What a wonderful place your home would be! And that is what this prayer is all about!

It's hard to imagine a more relevant prayer for your family than these lines by the apostle Paul. Make Paul's prayer for the believers in Ephesus your prayer for yourselves and your family and then watch God work to bring harmony to your home.

Prayer

Father God, You know the tensions in our family and You know where we fail to love each other. We earnestly pray that You would work in our hearts to root and establish us in Your love. Help each one of us realize how wide, how long, how high, and how deep Your love for us is. We pray this together and for our family, that we may glorify You in our home. Amen.

Taking Action

- Make a point of telling each member of your family today that you love him/her.

- Then do something to show a member of your family that you love him/her.
- Hugs are therapeutic. Your family members will be better at expressing love if they receive at least one hug a day. Get to work!

Reading On

Ephesians 4:29   Proverbs 24:3,4
James 1:22,23   James 2:15-17

Don't let what you cannot do interfere with what you can do.

—*John Wooden*

Know Your Children

Scripture Reading: Proverbs 22:1-16
Key Verse: Proverbs 22:6

> *Train a child in the way he should go, and when he is old he will not turn from it.*

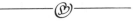

As we look at our grandchildren, Christine, Chad, Bevan, Bradley Joe II, and Weston Vaughn, we see five unique people and find ourselves face-to-face with the challenge of understanding each of them so that we can help mold godly character in them. Fortunately, each of them wants to be known. In fact, each one of us—whatever our age—wants people to take time to know us, to appreciate how we're different from everyone else, and to recognize our likes, our dislikes, and the things about us that make us who we are.

In raising our own children, Emilie and I saw a lot of differences between Jenny and Brad, and those differences are still there. Recognizing these differences early on, we realized that we had to teach, motivate, and discipline each of them according to their personality. God helped us understand that children need to be trained in a way tailor-made for them personally.

The first word in today's key verse is the word "train." In the Hebrew, this word originally referred to the roof of the mouth and the gums. In Bible times, the midwife would stick her finger into a sweet substance and then place it into the new baby's mouth to get the infant sucking. She would then hand the child to its mother, and the child would start nursing. This was the earliest form of "training." We need to keep in mind, though, that the word "child' in today's text can be a newborn up through a person of marrying age. The trick to get the baby nursing was only the first step in a long period of training.

And, according to the verse, the value of this training is so that "when he is old he will not turn from it." In Hebrew, this word for "old" means "bearded" or "chin." Solomon is talking about a young man who begins to grow a beard, and that can be as early as junior high or as late as college. The idea Solomon communicates is that we parents are to continue training our children as long as they are under our care—and we are to train our children God's way, not according to our ideas, our ways, or our plans.

It's important to see that this verse is not a guarantee to parents that raising children God's way means that they will never stray from His path. But our efforts to train our children to follow God will be most effective when we use the methods most appropriate to their unique personality. We need to approach each child differently and not compare them to one another. We need to appreciate the fact that each child is uniquely made. We need to be a student of our children.

It was easy to see that Jenny was not Brad and that Brad certainly wasn't Jenny. And like Jenny and Brad, each child has his or her own bent, already established by our Creator God when He places them in our family. God has given you unique children. Get to know them.

Prayer

Father God, thank You for the children You have placed in our care. Help us to know each of them well. Give us insight into their unique personalities, patience so we can understand them, and wisdom to know how to teach them. Help us to build them up to be all that You designed them to be. Amen.

Taking Action

- In what ways are your children different from you? Different from each other? Be specific.

- In light of the differences between your children you've identified, how will you train them differently? What approach will you take with each?

- Learn one new thing about each of your children today. Then do something with that information.

- Tell your child today one thing you appreciate about him/her that makes him/her special to you.

Reading On

Psalm 139:13-16

Be Still

Scripture Reading: Psalm 46: 1-11

Key Verse: Psalm 46:10

> *Be still, and know that I am God; I will be exalted among the nations, I will be exalted in the earth.*

———————— ✆ ————————

"Be still and know that I am God." Easier said than done, isn't it? It's hard to find a quiet moment in the day, a few minutes to relax and think and pray. We're constantly on the move, pressured by the demands of work and family and whatever church involvement, community activities, or recreation we try to fit in. Still moments with God just don't happen with full schedules. So what's the answer? Emilie and I have found that we have to make appointments with ourselves if we are to have a chance to rest, plan, regroup, and draw closer to God— and the same is probably true for you.

As I write these words, we are at a retreat in Laguna Beach, California. It's July, and the temperature is 83 degrees. The weather is perfect, and there's something calming about the waves crashing on the shore. We've spent four days resting and reading. This afternoon, we've talked about family, ministry, food, goals, God's love, His Word, and our writing. Now we're both quiet, and I'm feeling that rare sense of stillness that the psalmist talks about.

It's not often I'm still like this. My life isn't in balance the way I think it should be. I'm still more outwardly focused than inwardly focused. Goals and deadlines, coping with stress, taking care of daily chores, working toward retirement, getting things done—I spend more time and energy on these things than I do praying, meditating on God's Word, listening for His direction, dreaming, and just being with God.

When I was younger, my life was even more out of balance, but as I've gotten older, I find myself doing more of the inward things. I want to glorify God with my life. I want to spend more time alone with Him. I want to get to know Him better, I want Him to use me, and I want to know His peace. And you probably want those things for yourself as well. After all, regular down times—the psalmist's stillness—are as important and necessary as sleep, exercise, and healthy food. But, again, who has the time?

Well, Satan sure doesn't want us to take the time to be still with God. And he doesn't make it easy for us to eliminate the distractions of the job, stress from the boss, family responsibilities, ringing phones, and doing what the kids need. Emilie and I know the battle to make time for rest. So when we set up the year's calendar, we set aside blocks of time to be alone and quiet. In between the speaking engagements, interviews, and travel, we make time for quiet. Our marriage needs it. Our walk with God needs it.

Emilie talks about the door to stillness. And she's right. It's there waiting for any of us to open, but it won't open by itself. We have to choose to turn the knob and make time to enter and sit awhile. Each one of us needs to learn to balance the time we spend in quiet and calm with the time we spend in the fray of everyday existence. Ecclesiastes 3:1 says, "There is a time for everything"— and that includes a time to be still despite our busy life.

Prayer

Father God, life is moving much too fast. The demands never let up and the pressures never ease. We struggle to take a time out. We know we're more relaxed and can better serve You as husbands, wives, and workers when we have a daily time with You. Show us how to make that time happen. Amen.

Taking Action

- Read Ecclesiastes 3. What time in life is it for you right now?

- What will you do to cut down the busyness of your life? What distractions will you eliminate?

Reading On

Isaiah 30:15   Psalm 116:7

Notes

1. Source unknown.
2. Hyatt Moore, Wycliffe Bible Translators (Huntington Beach, CA., March 1995). Adapted from a newsletter.
3. Author unknown.
4. Author unknown.
5. Bill Bright, "Four Spiritual Laws" (Arrowhead Springs, CA: Campus Crusade for Christ International, 1965).
6. Elon Foster, *6000 Sermon Illustrations* (Grand Rapids, MI: Baker Book House, 1992), p. 624.
7. Books by Marilyn Willett Heavilin (published by Thomas Nelson): *Roses in December, Becoming a Woman of Honor, When Your Dreams Die, December's Song, I'm Listening, Lord.*
8. This resource is available through "Family Life Today," the radio program of Family Life, a ministry of Campus Crusade for Christ. To order call 1-800-FL-TODAY (1-800-358-6329).
9. Oswald Chambers, *My Utmost for His Highest* (Westwood, NJ: Barbour and Company, Inc.), p. 50.
10. Larry Crabb, *The Marriage Builder* (Grand Rapids, MI: Zondervan, 1982), pp. 105-06.
11. Gigi Graham Tchividjian, *Women's Devotional Bible, NIV Version*, (Grand Rapids: The Zondervan Corporation, 1990), p. 1307.
12. Bruce Narramore, *You're Someone Special* (Grand Rapids, MI: Zondervan Publishers, 1978), adapted from pp. 61-62.
13. Phyllis Hobe, *Coping* (Old Tappan, NJ: Fleming H. Revell Company, 1983), p. 46.
14. *"How God Taught Me to Give,"* (Wheaton, IL: Good News Publishers) Publishers and Distributors of Tract Literature.
15. Adapted from a tract published by Good News Publishers, Wheaton, IL.
16. Lana Bateman, *Poems for the Healing Heart* (Uhrichville, OH: Barbour & Company, 1992), p. 31.
17. Wilson Harrrell, "Making the Grade," in *Reader's Digest*, May 1995, p. 46.
18. Source unknown.
19. Bob Benson, *Laughter in the Walls* (Nashville, TN: Impact Books, 1969).
20. Elon Foster, *6000 Sermon Illustrations* (Grand Rapids, MI: Baker Book House, 1992), p. 309.
21. Adapted from Elon Foster, *6000 Sermon Illustrations* (Grand Rapids, MI: Baker Book House, 1992), p. 511.
22. Jerry and Barbara Cook, *Choosing to Love* (Ventura Books, 1982), p. 78-80.
23. Taken from a tract printed and distributed by the American Tract Society, Garland, Texas.
24. James Dobson, *The Strong-Willed Child* (Wheaton, IL: Tyndale House Publishers, 1971), p. 30.

Notes

25. James Dobson, *Hide and Seek*, rev. ed. (Old Tappan, N.J: Fleming H. Revell Co. , 1979), p. 95.

26. Patrick Morley, *The Man in the Mirror* (Brentwood, TN: Wolgemuth & Hyatt, 1989), pp. 5-7.

27. Source unknown.

28. Lee Iacocca, *Talking Straight* (New York: Bantam, 1988), p. 17.

29. Larry Crabb, *The Marriage Builder* (Grand Rapids, MI: Zondervan, 1982), p. 22.

30. Patrick Morley, *The Man in the Mirror* (Brentwood, TN: Wolgemuth Hyatt, 1989), adapted from pp. 12-14.

31. Sam Walton, *Sam Walton, Made in America* (New York: Doubleday, 1992), pp. 246-49.

32. Alan Loy McGinnis, *The Friendship Factor* (Minneapolis, MN: Ausburg Press, 1979), p. 14.

33. Stu Weber, *Locking Arms*, (Sisters, OR: Multnomah Books, 1995), p. 33.

34. Beth Wohlford, ed., Women's Ministry bulletin, Willow Creek Community Church, Barrington, IL, Sunday, August 27, 1995.

35. Stu Weber, *Locking Arms* (Sisters, OR: Multnomah Books, 1995), p. 251.

36. Ibid, pp. 50-51.

37. Adapted from Stephen R. Covey, *The Seven Habits of Highly Effective People* (New York: Simon and Schuster, 1989).

Harvest House Books by
Bob & Emilie Barnes

Bob & Emilie Barnes

*101 Ways to Love Your
    Grandchildren*
15-Minute Devotions for Couples
Good Manners for Today's Kids
Little Book of Manners for Boys, A
Simple Secrets Couples Should Know
Together Moments for Couples

Bob Barnes

15 Minutes Alone with God for Men
500 Handy Hints for Every Husband
5-Minute Bible Workouts for Men
5-Minute Faith Builders for Men
Five Minutes in the Bible for Men
*Old Guy's Guide to
    Living Young, An*
One Minute Alone with God for Men
What Makes a Man Feel Loved

Emilie Barnes

101 Ways to Clean Out the Clutter
15 Minutes Alone with God
15 Minutes of Peace with God
15 Minutes with God for Grandma
15-Minute Organizer, The
*365 Things Every Woman Should
    Know*
365 Ways to Organize Everything

*500 Time-Saving Hints for Every
    Woman*
An Invitation to Tea
Emilie's Creative Home Organizer
Five Minutes in the Bible for Women
Good Manners for Every Occasion
Good Manners in Minutes
Heal My Heart, Lord
I Need Your Strength, Lord
In the Stillness of Quiet Moments
Journey Through Cancer, A
Keep It Simple for Busy Women
Let's Have a Tea Party!
Little Book of Manners
Meet Me Where I Am, Lord
Minute Meditations for Busy Moms
*Minute Meditations for Healing &
    Hope*
More Faith in My Day
More Hours in My Day
Quick-Fix Home Organizer, The
Quiet Moments Alone with God
Simple Secrets to a Beautiful Home
Survival for Busy Women
Tea Lover's Devotional, The
Twelve Teas® of Inspiration, The
Walk with Me Today, Lord
What Makes a Woman Feel Loved
You Are My Hiding Place, Lord
Youniquely Woman